THE SAVE YOUR HEART
WINE BOOK

FRANK JONES

The
Save Your Heart
Wine Book

Published in 1995 by
Stoddart Publishing Co. Limited
34 Lesmill Road
Toronto, Canada
M3B 2T6
Tel. (416) 445-3333
Fax (416) 445-5967

Stoddart Books are available for bulk purchase for sales promo-
tions, premiums, fundraising, and seminars. For
details, contact the **Special Sales Department**
at the above address.

Canadian Cataloguing in Publication Data

Jones, Frank, 1937–
The save your heart wine book

ISBN 0-7737-2906-2

1. Wine - Therapeutic use. 2. Wine and wine making.
3. Heart - Diseases - Prevention. I. Title.

RM256.J65 1995   615.8'54   C95-931226-9

Cover Design: James Ireland Design Inc.
Typesetting: Tony Gordon/Image One Productions Ltd.
Line Drawings: Ivor Jones

Printed and bound in the U.S.A.

*Stoddart Publishing gratefully acknowledges the support
of the Canada Council, the Ontario Ministry of Culture, Tourism, and Recreation,
Ontario Arts Council, and Ontario Publishing Centre in the development of writing
and publishing in Canada.*

CONTENTS

Preface
A PERSONAL NOTE

The idea for this book sprang from plain old curiosity — and some worrying personal concerns. I was fascinated when, as a result of a chance remark by a friend at lunch one day, I heard about new research showing that wine may have the power to prevent heart disease, as well as help us live longer.

What I learned in the course of several thousand miles of travel to see some of the leading experts in this new area of science only confirmed my original excitement. Millions, I now believe, could benefit from new knowledge about this most ancient of beverages.

I won't pretend, though, that my research was disinterested. Now in my fifties, I am at the age of maximum risk for a heart attack. And if there was anything I could do to significantly reduce that risk, I wanted to know about it.

If you're my age, you don't need to be told about the dangers of coronary heart disease, the twentieth century's number one killer. We've all seen contemporaries or family members struck down. Sometimes, indeed, I feel my life has been framed by this silent and so often fatal disease.

I had my first encounter with the disease one luminous summer's evening on a cricket field in England when I was twelve years old. I played for our village cricket team in Kent; we were at batting practice when suddenly the man coming up to bowl, a tall, thin fellow in his fifties with steel grey hair, stumbled and fell. He did not get up. Today someone might have known cardiopulmonary resuscitation (CPR) and saved him. But, after someone had run to phone for the ambulance, we stood in a helpless circle, not knowing what to do. He began snoring loudly. Sheep munched unconcerned on the marsh nearby; a thrush performed his evensong in the willows; and a man lay snoring away his life. He was gone before the ambulance came, and we all went home. But I never forgot the sound of his snoring.

Two years later, my father went into hospital for an ulcer operation. I arrived home one afternoon with two school friends. I hardly noticed the little car belonging to John Carter, the manager of my father's road construction firm, parked in the driveway. He met us at the door and said he would like to speak to me in private for a moment. It must have been a task he dreaded. As we walked along the stone path around the rose bed, he told me that my father had survived the operation but had died of a heart attack shortly after. He was fifty-two.

I learned from my father's death. He was a chain smoker; I never smoked. I always followed the latest medical advice on heart health. In the early 1970s, as a Canadian newspaper correspondent based in London, I was jogging every morning in Hurlingham Park, near our home in Fulham. Back in Canada, I took up daily swimming and occasional cycling — both exercises the least likely to cause damage to joint or muscle. And, luckiest of all, I was married to Ayesha, who weaned me from meat 'n' potatoes swimming in gravy, and onto the fruits and fresh vegetables, the lentils, and the curries with fish or minimal meat on which she had been reared in the Caribbean.

Then, after a few years, I began losing friends to the silent killer. Some losses were simply heartbreaking. John DeKraker, a humorous, financially savvy Dutchman with whom I had served on the board of directors of our company credit union in Toronto, was in the passenger seat, his wife at the wheel, coming out of the driveway when he had a heart attack and died. He had just celebrated his forty-eighth birthday. They had four children. He had a full life ahead of him. And then nothing.

Other friends were "lucky." Their coronary heart disease was caught in time and they had preventive operations. They described to me the horrors of intensive care. But none of this had prepared me for the death of my friend Gary Lautens. He was Canada's best-known humorist and millions turned to his column in the *Toronto Star* every day to read about his wife, Jackie, "the Love Goddess," and the vicissitudes of their family life. Then, one weekend, he died of a heart attack.

It wasn't simply that a great talent was gone. The truly shocking thing about Gary's death was that, although he was sixty-three, it was not in the cards. He walked to and from work every day (some eight kilometres in total), never smoked, ate moderately, enjoyed a warm relationship with his wife and children, and gave the impression of a man totally at ease with himself. And, as everyone remarked, *he never touched a drop!*

This is almost unheard of in the newspaper world. And he endured plenty of joshing from his friend, the former British soccer writer and drama critic at the *Toronto Sun*, Bob Pennington. Bob would always put a full glass of wine conspicuously in front of Gary's plate when they dined together. It would still be sitting there when Gary got up. Jackie told me later that her husband had been put off drinking for good when he had to clean up after two alcoholic sports writers with whom he worked at the outset of his career.

You could never say, of course, that if Gary had accepted Bob's hospitality, if he had been a moderate wine drinker, the outcome would have been any different. It's just that we all thought that in choosing not to drink, Gary had made another wise choice that should have helped protect him against that ultimate catastrophe. And we were mistaken.

In the course of writing this book, I have learned a great deal about some of our mistakes and attitudes towards drinking. A year ago I could not have written about them. It is only thanks to the people named below, who showed patience indeed in helping this slow student, that I was able to write it. They are experts in the fields of enology (the science of wine-making), epidemiology, alcohol education, coronary disease, and other fields of medical knowledge.

My gratitude to: Alex Karumanchiri, David Goldberg, George Soleas, Wells Shoemaker, Tony Aspler, Serge Renaud, Tom Whitehead, Andy Waterhouse, Ed Frankel, Bruce German, Linda Bisson, Terry Leighton, Leroy Creasy, Arthur Klatsky, Selwyn St. Leger, Curtis Ellison, Sir Richard Doll, Anatoly Langer, Moira and Martin Plant, and Michael Marmot.

Introduction
LIFE AFTER THE FRENCH PARADOX

One quiet Sunday evening in November 1991, in the space of only twenty minutes, the wine industries of Canada and the United States were hit by something akin to a tornado. The reverberations from that event are still being felt today wherever wine is made or consumed.

What happened was probably the single most dramatic demonstration of the power of television to influence consumer habits — and public health. That evening millions of North Americans tuned in to the most popular U.S. program on the air, the CBS newsmagazine *60 Minutes*. And they learned for the first time about an anomaly called the "French Paradox." What they heard sent many scurrying to their liquor and wine stores. By the end of the week, sales of red wine were up 40 percent, fracturing for good the long-standing North American preference for sweeter white wines.

And the nature of the paradox? The French, especially those living in southwest France, defy all the health rules by smoking lots of Galois, exercising sparingly, and eating wicked amounts of saturated fats. Yet they have one of the lowest heart attack rates in the world. Scotland has among the highest heart attack rates in the world; a woman in Glasgow, for example, is twelve times more likely to die of a heart attack than a woman in Toulouse, France. And Canadian and American men are nearly three times as likely to die of heart attacks as those rugged guys from Toulouse.

The French appetite for red wine and a diet that includes lots of fresh fruit and vegetables were cited as the likely reasons for the paradox. Dr. Serge Renaud, the French doctor who identified the French Paradox, believes that red wine is the most powerful drug yet discovered in preventing coronary heart disease!

Wine — wisely chosen and consumed regularly and moderately — will help you to live longer. It's as simple as that. The ancients knew it: "Drink no longer water but use a little wine for thy stomach's sake, and thine own infirmities," St. Paul advised Timothy. And every month seems to bring new scientific evidence to strengthen the case.

Some of that evidence flies in the face of what most of us grew up believing. However, following studies from the last decade, there is no longer any doubt at all that abstainers are at greater risk of dying young than are moderate drinkers. And in the case of coronary heart disease — which claims the lives of more men and women in Canada and the United States than any other disease — a moderate alcohol intake (usually meaning two drinks or less a day) will reduce your chances of having a heart attack by 40 percent.

That's true whether you drink beer, wine, or liquor. It's related simply to the alcohol in the drinks, which boosts the "good" cholesterol in your blood, reduces the "bad" cholesterol, and cuts down the chances of a heart-stopping blood clot. But, starting with a breakthrough study in 1978 that showed heart attack figures are lowest in the countries where wine is the main drink, the case has been building steadily that wine is best.

Then in May 1995, Danish researchers came up with a startling finding: drinking wine regularly gave far and away the greatest protection, not only against fatal heart attacks, but against other mortal illnesses too. They had closely examined the lives of thirteen thousand citizens of Copenhagen over a twelve-year period. The wine drinkers in their study group were 60 percent less likely to die of a heart attack or a stroke, and 50 percent less likely to die from other illnesses.

The news had enormous significance in the prevention of atherosclerosis — the gradual clogging of the arteries that causes so many premature deaths. Wine, and red wine in particular, goes to work defending the body on two fronts. The alcohol it contains reduces harmful cholesterol and clotting agents, while powerful substances in the wine called antioxidants battle illness and even the aging process. The other secret of the French Paradox relates to *how* wine is consumed. Unlike beer or spirits, it is generally drunk slowly and with food. The world, it seems, has much to learn from the legendary French midday meal, eaten invariably in leisurely fashion and with the bottle ready at hand.

All of the above is extremely good news. You would expect to hear it shouted from the rooftops. If doctors discovered a drug that reduced the incidence of cancers by 40 percent, it would be an occasion for huge rejoicing. And cardiovascular disease — including the overwhelming proportion of strokes that are caused by hardening of the arteries — is more lethal than cancer.

Happily, the number of people dying prematurely of this twentieth-century plague is on the decline in most developed countries. That's because we're eating better, getting more exercise, and smoking less. But cardiovascular diseases still account for 40 percent of deaths in North America. And for women in the United States, the last few years have brought a disquieting new trend; their death rate is on the increase again after several years of decline. A 10 percent, let alone a 20 percent, reduction in heart attack and stroke rates resulting from sensible advice to drink a glass or two glasses of wine a day would be the best possible news. Not just as a statistic, but in human terms — in terms of fathers who would see their children grow up, mothers who would live to see their grandchildren.

Yet doctors have been strangely silent on the issue. Hardly anyone in the medical establishment is echoing St. Paul's advice to drink a little for your infirmities. If I've heard it once in the course of the research for this book, I've heard it a hundred times: "We can't possibly advise members of the public to drink for the sake of their health, even in moderation. It would be too dangerous."

In other words, you are not to be trusted.

You can feel a certain sympathy for the medical profession. A lot of what our mothers told us is true. Alcohol in excess is bad news. It leads to significant absenteeism and accidents at work, violence in the home, death or injury on the roads, and, for the persistent heavy drinker, the possibility of a stroke, cirrhosis of the liver, or certain cancers. And what doctor, after advising that alcohol is good for the heart, wants to pick up the newspaper and discover that someone has taken his advice too much to heart, gone on a binge, got behind the wheel, and killed somebody? There is also the question of the doctor's legal liability if things go wrong — especially in the United States where patients or their families are ever ready to sue.

So the furthest the medical profession will go is to say that it is okay for cardiologists or family doctors, in the privacy of their offices, to advise patients who have either had heart attacks, show symptoms of coronary heart disease, or have major risk factors in their background to drink in moderation. Yet there is a huge flaw in this thinking. Atherosclerosis is not a sudden event, like breaking a leg. It is a process. Fatty deposits — the precursors of atherosclerosis — are observable in the arteries of children. Between the ages of thirty and fifty-five men essentially "lay down" the plaque that may kill them. Women historically were not considered at risk until they reached menopause, but women's lifestyles have changed, with more women smoking, and more women in the work force; there is now increasing concern about heart disease as it affects younger women.

By the time a patient ends up in the doctor's office or the hospital with symptoms or significant risk factors, it's getting late in the day. And that's not even counting the people who died of heart attacks before they even knew they had coronary heart disease. We know now that life is not simply a lottery with a pre-ordained number on our ticket telling us when our time is up. To a large extent we can choose how long we want to live and in what condition. The time is over for the old medicine. If we're smart, we don't sit around waiting for a disease to happen and then expect the doctor to save us with a new miracle drug or an incredible new operation. By then, even if the doctor saves us, we may well be condemned to a compromised existence.

Surveys everywhere show that health and longevity are not determined by the amount of medical care available, but rather by our income and education. We're talking about people with the sense to make sound decisions about things like smoking, diet, and exercise, and the income and leisure to follow through. The fact that you are reading this book suggests (1) that you had enough money to buy it or enough gumption to borrow it, and (2) that you have an informed interest in your own health. You are, if I may presume, not the sort of person who, told that moderate wine consumption protects your heart, will go out on a wild drinking spree on the theory that if a little is good, more must be better. You are to be trusted. This book was intended for you.

Of course, many readers will not need to be told that wine is good for them in order to continue enjoying it. They would agree with Louis Pasteur, the first scientist to seriously study wine, who said, "A meal without wine is like a day without sunshine." Others, occasional or even nondrinkers, may have heard reports about the benefits of moderate drinking, particularly of red wine, and will want to know more. (At this point, there are no definitive brand-by-brand numbers available to identify the individual wines that offer the best protection. Instead I'll be offering guidelines on grape categories and regions, as well as suggesting wines that fit the formula.)

If this were just a book about wine — or beer or spirits for that matter — we could get straight away into discussing cuvées or the merits of Belgian versus German brews or the joys of single malts. But this book is really about health. Which is why considerable space is given to the risks as well as to the proven benefits of drinking for the sake of your health. And if it comes down on the side of the benefits, it is not only because I am confident that most people, in spite of what some experts say, are sensible drinkers, but also because heart disease is the larger tragedy. For people in the developed countries, it is with us all our lives, an inevitable consequence of our diet, smoking, and sedentary lifestyle.

Yet after learning about the French Paradox, I must admit that I wasn't one of those who acted right away. I was intrigued, but I suppose I thought the paradox was one of those anomalies that would eventually have a simple explanation. Perhaps it was something in the water. Then, one day in the summer of 1994, I was on the way to lunch in Toronto with my friend Alex Karumanchiri when I asked him casually, "When are you going to retire, Alex?" Alex, who was fifty-seven at the time, is head of quality control at the Liquor Control Board of Ontario

(LCBO) — the government monopoly that controls the sale of spirits and wine in Canada's most populous province. The board is the single largest purchaser of wine in the world, and its laboratories, under Alex's direction, enjoy a global reputation for the watchdog function they perform. "I'd like to retire," he replied, "but I'm involved in something so exciting I want to see it through." Alex was testing the phenolics in hundreds of wines from all over the world to determine their antioxidant potential. Antioxidants? Phenolics? It sounded like another language to me. I had only the most tenuous understanding of what he was talking about, but if it involved a 40 percent reduction in coronary heart disease risk, I wanted to hear about it.

That's how I got started on this book. I had a long road to travel before I ended up back at Alex's lab — to London, Oxford, Edinburgh and Dundee, California, and Boston. I had to learn about atherosclerosis, alcohol, and wine. I met with such experts as Serge Renaud and some of the foremost wine researchers at the University of California in Davis. Everywhere I received only help and consideration as my education proceeded. And everywhere I heard the same thing: drinking wine in moderation will indeed help to protect you against coronary heart disease and other diseases.

Professor David Goldberg, a physician and biochemist at the University of Toronto, puts it plainly: "If every adult North American drank two glasses of wine each day, cardiovascular disease, which accounts for almost 50 percent of deaths in this population, would be cut by 40 percent and $40 billion could be saved annually." But drinking wine for your health is not the first, nor even the second, thing you should do to beat the mortality odds. Giving up smoking is the single best thing anyone can do to live longer. Reducing your consumption of eggs, dairy products, red meat, and other fatty foods, and sinking your teeth into lots of fresh fruit and vegetables will go a long way towards improving your chances of dodging the silent killer. Regular exercise too needs to become part of your life. After that — and if the balance of risks and benefits you'll read about here is in your favour — you should, I'll say it clearly, consider drinking wine regularly and moderately for the health of your heart and to live longer.

CHAPTER I

The Truth
About Alcohol

DRINKING AND HEALTH: THE UNAVOIDABLE TRUTH

If anyone else had said it, it wouldn't have mattered nearly as much. But the white-haired, slightly stooped figure at the conference room podium of the Hotel Inter-Continental in Sydney, Australia, was billed as "the world's leading epidemiologist." Sir Richard Doll (now emeritus professor of medicine at Oxford University) had been the first scientist to put his finger definitively on the link between smoking and lung cancer. Fifty-two years later, in October 1991, Sir Richard was ready to make another important pronouncement. After carefully reviewing the mounting evidence, he told delegates at the Medicinal Virtues of Alcohol in Moderation Conference: "I conclude that light or moderate consumption of alcohol reduces the risk of coronary disease."

Regular consumption of up to four drinks a day, he said, may reduce the risk of coronary heart disease by as much as 50 percent. He was prepared to go further: "This scientific evidence must, I think, be interpreted as indicating that both men and women who regularly drink small amounts of alcohol tend to have a lower morbidity and mortality from coronary disease and a lower mortality from *all causes combined* than those who permanently abstain." (my emphasis)

In other words, moderate drinking not only protects you from coronary heart disease, but it also decreases the chances that you will die from other diseases. This protection against all-cause mortality was evident at drinking levels of up to two drinks of wine, beer, or spirits a day. For Sir Richard Doll, by nature a cautious man, to make such an emphatic statement meant there was really very little room left for argument. It was a fact: while excessive drinking was a risk factor for many diseases, abstaining was almost equally dangerous. Moderate drinkers were the ones who could expect to live longest.

Another scientist at the same conference, Dr. Charles Hennekens, professor of preventative medicine at Harvard, estimated that in Britain alone a 20 percent reduction in deaths from coronary heart disease resulting from moderate alcohol use would mean twenty to forty thousand lives saved annually.

It had taken sixty-five years for the truth about alcohol to be accepted. In 1926, an American biologist named Raymond Pearl reported that people who drank moderate amounts of alcohol lived longer than people who didn't drink at all. He was the first to enunciate the U-shaped curve that today is accepted almost as a rule of nature wherever health and alcohol consumption are debated.

It works like this: nondrinkers are used as the baseline; they have a 1.00 risk of dying of coronary heart disease. But for those who have a couple of drinks a week, the risk is slightly less, maybe 0.90. In other words, their chance of dying of coronary heart disease is only 90 percent that of the abstainer dying. As the consumption increases, up to maybe two or three drinks a day, the benefit increases and the risk drops to perhaps 0.70 or 0.60. But after that, as consumption increases, the mortality line starts to curve upwards, passing the baseline again and becoming progressively steeper. What it amounts to is that abstaining is a health risk; moderate drinking is good for you, but heavy drinking is very bad indeed. Moderate amounts of alcohol will provide a quite significant measure of protection against coronary heart disease, and even relatively heavy drinkers are still largely protected against it. But, as their consumption rises, they are much more likely to die from certain cancers, hemorrhagic stroke (the less common kind), liver cirrhosis, suicide, and accident. Although the risk profile is generally described as U-shaped, it's more accurate to call it J-shaped because the risk for heavy drinkers rises so steeply.

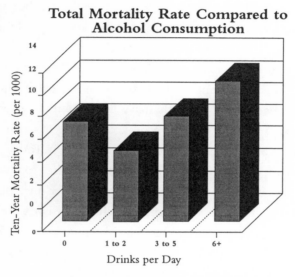

Total Mortality Rate Compared to Alcohol Consumption

Adapted from Klatsky et al., 1981

The prescient Raymond Pearl had no detailed evidence of this; all he knew was that light drinkers were less likely to die than teetotallers. Twelve years later Pearl came up with another finding: death rates for smokers went up in a straight line. Unlike alcohol, there was no benefit for light smokers. But no one wanted to listen, either about alcohol or cigarettes, and for decades Pearl's findings were forgotten — in the case of alcohol, not merely forgotten, but deliberately ignored. Information that moderate amounts of alcohol might be good for you was disturbing to North America's zealous temperance movement, which was largely religion-inspired.

In recent decades, the temperance flag has been handed to bureaucrats at the national and international level who, with a great deal of justification, have waged war on the undoubted social and medical ills caused by excessive alcohol consumption. The trouble is that, in their zeal to do good, many are determined that any favourable news about alcohol must be suppressed — even if it has the potential for saving lives. Their message is: "Don't confuse the public."

Dr. Curtis Ellison, a cardiologist and epidemiologist at Boston University School of Medicine, tells me that until quite recently there was "a gentleman's agreement" that scientists would not apply for U.S. government funding for projects that were likely to show alcohol in a favourable light. Today projects occasionally slip through if they treat alcohol — usually wine — as part of the diet, rather than focusing on just the drink itself. The situation may improve further. Early in 1995, Congress mandated the U.S. Health and Human Services Department to fund research into the health benefits of alcohol, and wine in particular. It remains to be seen whether the new tight-fisted Republican majority will block that initiative.

In Canada, too, it is still easier to get funding for projects related to the evils of alcohol than it is to get support for research into alcohol or wine's health benefits. For generations, in fact, doctors tended to equate alcohol only with disease and death. "Alcohol studies" invariably meant looking at the bleak side of the equation — drinking and driving, cirrhosis, and various forms of unpleasant death. For that reason, many of the doctors involved in the early research on alcohol's health benefits were cautious in announcing their findings.

But if Sir Richard Doll is the scientist who finally made the topic respectable in Europe, in North America it was Dr. Arthur Klatsky, one of this continent's most respected cardiologists, who significantly turned the tide. Klatsky, who looks like one of Santa Claus's bearded elves, works at the Kaiser Permanente Medical Center in Oakland, California, where 2.5 million people are registered as patients. He told me that, around 1970, he and colleague Dr. Gary Friedman began sifting through computer records to identify traits predictive of heart disease. In one exercise they matched five hundred patients who had suffered heart attacks with five hundred patients of similar age who hadn't.

"It was a fishing expedition," he said, smiling. "We had no hypothesis about drinking."

When alcohol was indicated as having a protective effect, he was skeptical: "I attacked the hypothesis from every possible viewpoint." Before publishing a paper on their findings in 1974, he gave it to his wife, Eileen, to read. "She's my most honest critic, and she said, 'It's almost as if you don't believe this, or don't want to believe it.'" Klatsky admits, "We were worried about how it would be received." Klatsky and Friedman persisted, expanding their studies to cover 85,000 subjects, and then 124,000 and 129,000. And the answer was always the same: light to moderate drinking protected against coronary heart disease. And soon scientists all over the world were coming up with similar findings:

❲ In 1976 researchers in Hawaii, studying 7,705 Japanese men in Honolulu, found alcohol substantially reduced the risk for coronary heart disease as well as heart attacks. Four years later, the same team reported moderate alcohol consumption also reduced the risk of death from cancer and ischemic stroke (the type resulting from an artery blockage).

❲ In Australia in 1982, the Busseltown study showed moderate drinkers who didn't smoke had the lowest heart attack rates.

❴ In 1986 the ongoing Framingham, Massachusetts, heart study revealed a classic U-shaped curve among 2,100 males and 2,600 females followed at that point for twenty-four years. Light drinkers were 70 percent less likely to have a heart attack than abstainers.

❴ The huge American Cancer Society study of 277,000 men reported in 1990 that not only did one drink a day reduce coronary heart disease risk by 25 percent, but moderate drinkers were also slightly less likely to die of cancer than abstainers.

But perhaps the most remarkable piece of evidence to emerge resulted from a New Zealand study led by Professor Rodney Jackson and published in 1992, which looked at both men and women. The general belief at that time had been that moderate alcohol consumption provides a sort of low-level, background protection against coronary heart disease. Many doctors, however, still believed that drinking episodes might actually provoke a heart attack in the ensuing twenty-four hours by upsetting the rhythm of the heart. Jackson and his team matched men and women who had experienced fatal or nonfatal heart attacks with people from the general population of similar age and sex. Using ingenious measuring methods, they established that it was people who had consumed alcohol in the previous twenty-four hours who were least likely to have a heart attack. Surprisingly, women seemed better protected than men. A woman, for example, who had had four or more drinks in the previous twenty-four hours reduced her chances of having a heart attack by half compared with a female abstainer. In other words, alcohol provided immediate and substantial protection.

In all there have been some sixty studies; in reviewing them, researchers in Britain and the United States concluded there could no longer be any argument about the existence of the U-shaped curve. The major debate then switched from the existence of a benefit for moderate drinkers to the level of drinking at which the maximum benefit was achieved. The estimates ranged from less than one drink a day to three to five drinks a day.

Until the early 1990s, Dr. Klatsky had been cautious about giving any *general* endorsement to the idea that moderate alcohol consumption was good for you. And he still has legitimate concerns about the wrong people taking up drinking.

> If the person is a nondrinker, I always try to ascertain why that is. Most have a good reason, like an antipathy to alcohol, or a religious reason, or a personal history of a drinking problem. Then I urge them to remain nondrinkers.
>
> But I've seen people who have had heart trouble, and who have decided to give up a moderate drinking habit because they believe everything enjoyable in life must be bad for you. I tell them they've made a mistake, that they would be better off being light drinkers instead of abstainers.

If, as happens commonly, the patient's only risk factor is low levels of "good" cholesterol (see Chapter II), and alcohol in moderation boosts "good" cholesterol, "I may encourage that person, whether a middle-aged man or woman, to have one drink a day as a prescription. And I must say I really do not honestly believe anybody that I have ever advised [to drink] has become a heavy drinker."

Klatsky had a very personal reason for becoming a cardiologist: heart disease runs in his family. "My father died of coronary disease in his sixties, his brother earlier than that, and so on . . . I've tried to follow a proper lifestyle, avoiding smoking, staying thin, and exercising conscientiously." And, he added, he drinks a glass of wine with dinner every night.

By 1993 Dr. Klatsky felt the time had come to speak out. With Friedman, he wrote a landmark editorial in the influential *New England Journal of Medicine* (NEJM), announcing: "There now seems little doubt that alcohol exerts a protective effect against coronary heart disease. Most large-scale studies have shown that people who consume one or two drinks a day have fewer coronary events than abstainers." The evidence, they wrote, came from "large, well-controlled studies in diverse populations and settings."

There had only been one major hiccup in the steady acceptance of this once very controversial idea. In 1988, Professor Gerry Shaper led a team at the Royal Free Hospital School of Medicine, in London, England, reporting on seven thousand men, aged forty to fifty-nine, taking part in the British Regional Heart Study. They found the familiar U-shaped curve, and the maximum protective benefit from coronary heart disease came at two to four drinks per day, at which level the men were 50 percent less liable to die of coronary artery disease than abstainers.

Professor Shaper, however, had a different explanation for these dramatic figures. It was quite possible, he argued, that this and other studies were flawed by the fact that the "abstainers" included former drinkers who, because of heart and other problems, had been forced to give up drinking. It would be only natural that these "sick-quitters," as Shaper called them, would succumb early to coronary disease, thus skewing the figures and making it look as if abstainers were at much greater risk than they really were. It was an intriguing idea, and it prompted the influential *Lancet* to declare the U-shaped curve "a myth."

Shaper's theory interested Sir Richard Doll in the alcohol controversy, and on a windy October day in 1994, dodging Oxford's lethal student cyclists, I made my way to the world-famous Radcliffe Infirmary to hear about it. Sir Richard, eighty-two when I spoke to him, first led me from his modest office to a staff room where he made me a cup of coffee. It was after reading Shaper's theory, said Sir Richard, "that we realized we had data which could answer this conclusively."

In 1951 thirty-four thousand British doctors had been enrolled in a study on the effects of cigarette smoking on health. In 1978, in a study Sir Richard conducted with Professor Richard Peto, some twelve thousand of those still surviving were asked to test the protective effects of aspirin against coronary heart disease. The study had nothing to do with alcohol, but just to make sure that drinking wouldn't be a confounding factor, the doctors, all male and over forty-five, were asked to record their drinking habits.

The reason the figures from the thirteen-year aspirin study were important now, Sir Richard continued, was that the doctors taking part had been asked detailed questions about their vascular history and about any previous heart disorders. And, being physicians, their answers were likely to be accurate. It was finally possible to separate bona fide abstainers from "sick-quitters." The figures from the aspirin study were reworked, and the U-shaped curve for alcohol emerged, as usual, intact. The maximum protective benefit was found at a level of one to two drinks a day.

There were delays in getting figures from the doctors' study published, and in the meantime several other studies had gone a long way towards answering Shaper's criticism. "But I think our paper has just put the lid on it," said Sir Richard, with a mischievous twinkle. "Even Shaper now accepts that the reduction (in heart disease) in light drinkers cannot be explained by people giving up drinking because of heart disease."

Sir Richard, who describes himself as "a moderate drinker," and who has wine with dinner every night (as well as enjoying an occasional Ruddles beer), is now firmly convinced of the benefits of moderate drinking. Coronary heart disease and ischemic stroke, the most common form of stroke, are both related to clogged arteries, and both cause a substantial proportion of deaths among the middle-aged and elderly, he says. "Reductions in their mortality of up to 50 percent far outweigh the increased risks of cancer, cirrhosis, and injury caused by small amounts of alcohol."

Just how important is moderate drinking on the scale of things you can do to ward off coronary heart disease? "Stopping smoking is more important," he replied. "If you smoke, there's nothing you can do which will get the risk down to that of a nonsmoker." As for other factors, "It's a toss-up between alcohol and [a proper] diet. The reduction in risk you can achieve from alcohol is really quite substantial, probably 40 percent. But a sensible diet [as well] will certainly take the risk lower. Nobody has tested really what the effect of exercise is, but I would expect it to have an increased benefit."

And what does he say to alcohol education groups who want to downplay the health benefits of wine and alcohol so as not to give the public a confusing message about drinking?

"You must treat people as adults," he replied. "They are entitled to the facts. Once you start withholding facts because it makes education difficult, where do you stop?"

How Alcohol Works

How does alcohol work? Why is it that moderate drinkers experience less coronary heart disease, fewer heart attacks, and fewer ischemic strokes than abstainers?

Picture this common scenario. Carl the Cabdriver pulls in to Fat Sam's for his Great Canadian Lunch: the Big Daddy cheeseburger, large fries, and large Coke. His artery walls, already showing multiple rents and tears from twenty years of smoking and bulging with plaque from his sedentary life behind the wheel and high-fat diet, groan under the fresh assault. The extra dollop of saturated fat may be enough to cause fresh injuries to the inflamed walls, and immediately fire bells, set off by chemicals called thromboxanes, are ringing. The blood platelets — the tiny disks that rush in to staunch the flow of blood when we cut ourselves — go into action. They, simple souls, think they're helping Carl. They crowd around the injury sites and bravely hold hands to form a net of protection. They release substances that signal other platelets to come to the rescue until a platelet plug is formed, causing a shortage of oxygen for the heart and possibly triggering rhythm disturbances.

"A-w-w!" groans Carl, clutching his chest. "Damn indigestion. Gimme some seltzer, will you, Sam?"

He may get away with it. Platelet plugs are fragile and not necessarily fatal. But now it gets messy. The platelets ooze a clotting agent that grabs the passing blood cells and causes them to form a clot. This gets into what the doctors call a "cascading" effect. Soluble circulating proteins gather at the trouble spot to form one great messy glob of jelly-like material. The very mechanisms Nature devised to protect Carl from cuts and infections have turned on him with a vengeance.

"Call an ambulance, Sam. I'm feeling weird." If Carl is lucky, he won't die on the spot of cardiac arrest. If his now compromised heart can keep beating, if somewhat feebly, until the ambulance crew can give him first aid and get him to the hospital, there's a good chance he'll survive. But he won't be driving his cab for a while and it's goodbye to the Great Canadian Lunch.

A smarter Carl would have given up smoking years ago, joined the health club, and ordered a fish sandwich and a salad for lunch. Just suppose too that every night Carl also had a glass of wine or a bottle of beer with his supper, plus an aspirin or half an aspirin in the morning for further protection. Then, when those warning bells went off, the drink he had the night before might have helped to defuse the whole crisis.

Alcohol — like aspirin — makes the platelets less sticky, less able to hold hands and form that dangerous obstruction. Research suggests that aspirin and moderate alcohol consumption work together to give even more protection than they do independently. In addition, small amounts of alcohol inhibit production of thromboxanes, the chemicals that were wildly signalling the platelets into action.

There are even more ways in which moderate amounts of alcohol, especially wine, are believed to intervene to prevent cardiac crises. Sometimes, simply because we're under stress, the white blood cells will secrete inflammatory chemicals called leukotrienes. Anti-inflammatory drugs can block the leukotrienes — but so can compounds called phenolics found in red wine.

In 1994 there was more good news. In the Netherlands, doctors found that older patients given wine with their dinner showed elevated levels of t-PA, an anti-clotting agent that, in artificial form, is used to save patients who have had a heart attack. A Harvard Medical School study of 631 healthy doctors aged forty to eighty-four also showed that regular, moderate drinkers had elevated t-PA levels. And if that doesn't do the trick, in other studies, alcohol has been shown to increase fibrinolysis, the process by which clots dissolve.

There are still two more beneficial effects thought to decrease the chances of heart attack or ischemic stroke: (1) moderate drinking relieves stress, another cause of coronary catastrophe; and (2) it relaxes the muscles in the arteries so that they don't contract, further constricting the flow channel. At just about every level of the frightening cascade that leads to the hospital emergency room and the defibrillator, alcohol, in moderate quantities, provides protection. Why then, I asked Dr. Michael Gaziano, a Boston cardiologist and researcher, are coronary heart disease levels in Scotland and Finland, both countries where elbow-bending is a popular national pastime, not at the lowest rather than the highest levels?

Smoking, lack of exercise, and bad diet are all part of the explanation, he replied. But there's more to it than that. In Italy, where his parents came from, which has one of the lowest coronary heart disease rates, "about 90 percent of the population have one drink a day. But northern Europe and North America are temperance societies where liquor is drunk for its mind-numbing effects. You do it to get a buzz on Saturday night."

In total alcohol consumed, the Italians are well ahead of Canadians, Americans, British, and Australians. But they do their drinking steadily and usually with meals. It's binge drinking — crowding all your drinking into the weekend instead of taking regular small amounts of alcohol — that does a lot of the harm, said Dr. Gaziano. Although moderate amounts of alcohol reduce the stickiness of the platelets, large amounts — Saturday night amounts — cause a rebound effect about eighteen hours later and actually increase the stickiness of the platelets. So you could be in trouble just about the time you're planning a nap after Sunday dinner.

Short-Term Effects of Alcohol Consumption (among regular drinkers)				
No. of drinks in last 24 hours	Odds Ratio* for Acute Myocardial Infarction		Odds Ratio* for Cardiac Death	
	Men	Women	Men	Women
None	1.0	1.0	1.0	1.0
1–2	0.73	0.59	0.61	0.60
3–4	0.67	0.81	0.57	0.52
>4	0.76	0.50	0.60	0.73
All drinkers	0.75	0.61	0.75	0.46

* Adjusted for age, smoking, and usual alcohol consumption.
Modified from Jackson et al., 1992

Exercise, good diet, and not smoking are vital to good heart health. But, as we have seen, alcohol in moderation is truly a wonder drug operating on a whole range of levels to see us safely through the middle years.

CHAPTER II

Living
Ourselves
to Death

You and Your Heart

It's the stillness that strikes you, the utter silence. No wonder they call this the silent killer. In their rooms, the patients lie quietly, contemplating their fears. Their shoulders are hunched — as if they are afraid that with any sudden movement they might break apart. This is the reality of coronary heart disease. It stalks us for decades without our knowing, and then we end up in one of these silent hospital rooms. Or worse.

The only movement I detected in the coronary care unit at St. Michael's Hospital in downtown Toronto was at the nursing station. On three television monitors, invisible electronic fingers recorded the heartbeats of the twelve patients in the acute beds in the unit. Nobody seemed to be paying any attention to the screens. "Don't worry," Dr. Anatoly Langer, the cardiologist in charge of the unit, reassured me. "If anything changes a beeper goes off. And we're pretty attuned in this department to hearing the beeper."

Half of the patients in the unit were recovering from heart attacks while the others had been admitted with chest pains or other suspicious symptoms. Typically the men here with heart attacks had been stricken with a crushing pain, "like an elephant sitting on my chest." It most likely happened in the first hours of the day, when the heart is under most pressure as it kick-starts the body into activity. For the women the symptoms of their heart failure might have been different and easier to ignore — like feeling nauseous and tired. The unit could easily have been in Melbourne or Aberdeen or Houston. These units, wherever you find them, are all the same. And there are rarely any empty beds.

CHD League Table for 1992
Mortality in Men and Women 40–69

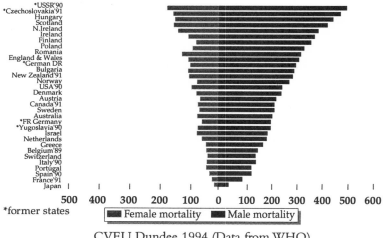

CVEU Dundee 1994 (Data from WHO)

Atherosclerosis — the gradual obstruction of the arteries that can lead to heart attack or stroke — has always been with us. It is only in this century, though, that it has reached epidemic proportions. We are living ourselves to death. "It reached its peak in the 1950s and 1960s," Professor David Goldberg, the University of Toronto biochemist, told me. "It's the price we're paying for our modern living style. We are living much more sedentary lives, and we're eating more artificial as opposed to natural foods, including a lot of fats."

The message, though, is finally getting through. People are exercising more, eating better, smoking less, and coronary heart disease as well as strokes are on the decline in most countries. Some decline! In Canada cardiovascular diseases — heart attacks and strokes — kill seventy-seven thousand people a year, and in the United States the figure is close to a million.

Certain groups are at special risk. In Canada cardiovascular disease accounts for 41 percent of all deaths, but for people whose roots are in the Indian subcontinent, the figure is 53 percent. In Britain, the death rate for men from that same region is 36 percent higher than for the indigenous population; for East Indian women it's 46 percent higher. In the United States the death rate for black men is 47 percent higher than for whites; for black women, 69 percent higher.

How does it happen, this devastating but invisible process?

Back in his tiny office at the hospital, Dr. Langer explained. When we are babies, the walls of our arteries are milky white and smooth as rubber. But the first traces of fat buildup have been observed in babies as young as ten months old. And, thanks to our fatty diet and early smoking patterns, it's normal now for pathologists to find the early signs of cholesterol buildup in the arteries of teenagers killed in accidents.

In the first half of life it's more of a problem for men than for women (although that may be changing). Men, said Dr. Langer, need to start worrying about coronary heart disease at thirty (the American Heart Association warns that atherosclerosis often makes rapid advances in the thirties), women usually at menopause. By the time those milky-smooth arteries of childhood have endured twenty or thirty or forty years of a Western diet rich in saturated fats and have been repeatedly assaulted by the toxins in tobacco smoke — either first or secondhand — without the respite that regular exercise provides, they are not a pretty sight. Under the microscope the artery walls appear as scarred and pitted as the face of the moon. In cross section the artery may resemble a half-closed eye — the passage through which the blood must pass now reduced to perhaps 30 or 40 percent of its original size by plaque buildup.

It is not simply a case of fatty cholesterol adhering to the sides of the arteries like pipes furring up. It is a much more dynamic process than that. Cholesterol is a soft, fatty substance that forms part of our cells and performs a number of chemical functions essential to life. Most, if not all, of the cholesterol we need is made by the liver, which churns out about 1,000 milligrams a day. But we often get more than we need from the fatty foods we eat. An easy way to think of it is this: foods from animals contain it; most foods from plants don't.

Because it's fatty, cholesterol cannot dissolve in the bloodstream: it needs to be carried around. It travels and is deposited in the cells in the form of a molecule consisting of fat and protein (lipoprotein). Lipoproteins come in two forms, having opposite functions. Low density lipoprotein (LDL), sometimes called "bad" cholesterol, is the delivery system bringing cholesterol to the cells; high density lipoprotein (HDL), "good" cholesterol, carries away the surplus, returning it to the liver for disposal. Ideally, the two are in balance and cholesterol does not accumulate.

For the sake of simplicity, and not to confuse us, the doctor will tell us we have "high" cholesterol or "low" cholesterol. Which is fair enough because the "bad" LDL cholesterol makes up the larger portion of the cholesterol in our blood. So a "high" combined figure is cause for concern. But if we want a more precise picture of what's happening in our arteries, we should ask the doctor about the ratio of HDL to LDL. The more "good" HDL there is in proportion to the "bad" LDL, the more effectively the fatty cholesterol is being moved back to the liver for disposal. Women, prior to menopause, naturally have high levels of HDL. Moderate intakes of alcohol also help to boost HDL levels in men and women.

High LDL levels are very bad news for the arteries. Over time, they lead to plaque buildup that may partially or totally block the blood flow. The process itself is vicious and multifaceted. The protective lining of the arteries, the endothelium,

Drinking and HDL Cholesterol

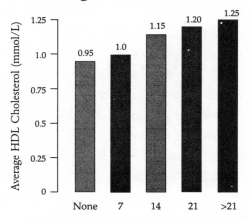

Average Number of Alcoholic Drinks per Week

is bombarded and pierced by oxidized LDL (a villain we'll learn more about in the section on antioxidants), also allowing white blood cells to penetrate and build up. Fatty streaks and foam cells help to thicken the artery walls, calcium accumulates (hence the "hardening" of the arteries), while inflammation and scar tissue further diminish the size of the channel through which the blood must force its way.

Is atherosclerosis reversible? In the last few years there has been a good deal of excitement in medical circles about drugs that actually seem to reverse the process. Dr. Langer advises we shouldn't hold our breath. The reduction is slow and slight: "It took fifty years to build up the plaque; it could take fifty years to remove it," he said.

As you go about your daily life, oblivious to these changes taking place inside, the results can be varied, modest, or downright alarming. There may be enough blood and oxygen getting through to the heart for normal purposes, and a deficit will only show up when you run or exert yourself — as you collapse into the seat after dashing for the train you'll feel a sharp pain in the chest. It's called angina or myocardial ischemia, and it's a useful warning for you that you could suffer a heart attack in the near future.

More alarming, because of arterial spasms or artery disease, many people will have small heart attacks without ever knowing it. This condition is called silent ischemia; the first you'll know about it is when you get a full-blown heart attack and, after testing, the doctor tells you it isn't your first. Exercise tests and continuous heart monitors are about the only way to detect these treacherous little episodes.

The heart attack proper is likely to occur when a piece of the gunge blocking your coronary arteries breaks off and forms an obstruction. Or else when a clot forms in the swirling eddies of the constricted channels, and the heart is in trouble. (If the obstruction occurs in the arteries leading to the brain, a stroke will be the consequence; if it occurs in the arteries leading to the arms and legs, then gangrene can result.) Deprived of oxygen, parts of that miraculous little muscle — no bigger than your clenched fist — may die or wildly irregular rhythms may lead the heart to stop altogether in sudden cardiac arrest. That is the fear that men especially carry in their middle years (women are still largely oblivious to the real dangers they face). It's a justified fear.

At the Royal Edinburgh Infirmary I had seen two bleak-looking and much-used resuscitation rooms where, using brute force and defibrillators, nurses and doctors try to pummel and shock hearts back into life. You will find such units in every modern hospital. At St. Mike's, as it's known affectionately, Dr. Langer showed me the super-sophisticated equipment that is available to diagnose and/or revive patients on the coronary floor. New drugs, bypass operations, angioplasty (the use of a balloon device to open up blocked arteries), and even ultrasound are only part of the plethora of techniques at the doctor's fingertips.

But all this assumes that you get to the hospital alive. The fact is that between 20 and 50 percent of people who have heart attacks — estimates vary — die before they get to the hospital. The worst thing is sudden cardiac arrest, which, as the name suggests, is the total stoppage of the heart. It accounts for about half of all cardiac deaths. If it happens to you at home or at work, your chances of being alive and well thirty days later are, according to Dr. Langer, about 5 to 10 percent. Even if you have cardiac arrest in hospital, with all the equipment and know-how at hand, your chances of leaving the hospital alive and well are only 10 to 20 percent.

If you survive that first heart attack, there's a 90 percent chance you will still be alive at the end of the year. But once you've had a heart attack, Dr. Langer told me, your life expectancy is likely to be shorter than if you hadn't.

These are the facts we don't generally hear. Instead we often read in the newspaper about people who have had heart attacks resuming full and busy lives, and even running in marathons. It's a bit of a fraud. Even though, according to the American Heart Association, 88 percent of those under sixty-five do return to work after surviving a heart attack, about two-thirds of heart attack victims don't make a full recovery.

Don't get me wrong. If I had a heart attack, or seemed in danger of having one, I would certainly prefer to be hooked up to the monitor with the best of care ready at hand. But that doesn't guarantee I won't have a heart attack or a stroke right there in my hospital bed and die.

Despite huge advances in what we know about the heart and the circulatory system, coronary heart disease is still largely a mystery: cardiologists are like anglers fishing with worms and bobbers on the surface of an ocean. Their main frustration comes from the fact that they generally arrive so late on the scene in the disease's progress. Our bodies generally give us no hint of the gradual buildup of plaque in our arteries.

Since 1948, the citizens of Framingham, Massachusetts, have been put under the microscope in one of the world's longest-running total health studies. One of its findings was that of those who died suddenly of cardiac arrest, half the men and two-thirds of the women had no previous symptoms. Sudden death is often the first sign of illness. Almost as alarming is the fact that as people age, the likelihood of their experiencing those silent heart attacks increases. The damage may be permanent and the patient isn't even aware of it. It's estimated that anywhere from 20 to 60 percent of all heart attacks fall in this category, and women are more susceptible than men. Dr. Langer, who has made a study of silent heart attacks, said often the patient simply doesn't notice symptoms like sweating or mild chest pain. Diabetics, who frequently are insensitive to pain, are especially vulnerable.

The sheer unpredictability of cardiac events is also deeply frustrating to cardiologists. "You may see a patient with only a 20 percent buildup one day and he'll have a 100 percent blockage the next," said Dr. Langer. "Other people with 50 to 60 percent blockage will live out their lives without anything happening. I can say that out of one hundred people like you, ten will die. But I can't tell you if you will be one of the ten."

One cardiologist I met likes to begin his talks by flashing up slides of Arthur Ashe, the 1975 Wimbledon tennis champion, alongside Sir Winston Churchill. Ashe, a super-fit athlete, did everything he could to stay in shape, but fell victim to heart disease, underwent surgery during which he received a tainted blood transfusion, and subsequently died of AIDS. Churchill smoked large cigars, stayed in bed until lunch, did not exercise, and ate a rich diet that defied all the health rules. He was also known to be fond of the bottle. He died at ninety-one.

WHY WOMEN SHOULD WORRY

Ask most women to name the biggest cause of death for women under sixty-five and, almost inevitably, the answer will be "breast cancer." The right answer: coronary heart disease.

In Canada cardiovascular diseases claim only slightly fewer women than men — 37,000 to 39,600 in 1992. The American Heart Association's latest statistical supplement for 1995 has a chilling graph. It shows cardiovascular death trends for men and women. The two lines crossed in 1984 and grew farther apart: the rate for women overtook that for men. Both rates continued to decline — until 1990, when the rate for women started to go up again.

There's a reason why, in the past, the heart problems of women got scant attention. Plaque starts to build up, generally, much earlier in men's arteries than in women's. Men start to get heart attacks at thirty-five. But women are usually protected by their hormones. Estrogen prevents the buildup of cholesterol. Only after menopause, when the estrogen supply dwindles, do cholesterol levels start to rise. One of the reasons women are advised to take an estrogen supplement after menopause is to reduce the chance of heart attack.

For men, essentially, coronary heart disease has been looked on as a mid-life threat. For women, the threat came later.

Cardiovascular Disease Mortality Trends
for Males and Females
United States: 1979-1991

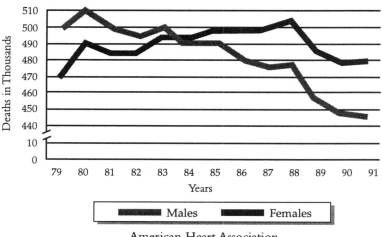

American Heart Association

The rule of thumb was that heart attacks came ten years later for women than for men. So perhaps it's not so surprising that, according to a number of studies, heart disease in men is treated much more aggressively by doctors than heart disease in women. To be callous about it, there is more pressure to save the life of a young father with perhaps thirty years of life ahead of him than there is to save a woman of seventy with a more limited outlook. Studies in several countries show women are less likely to be correctly diagnosed in the first place, and are less likely to get the drugs and the operations that could save their lives. And when a woman has a heart attack, she is more likely to die from it.

That's got to change. Heart disease is increasingly of concern to women in middle life. It's not hard to understand why: in many ways, women's lives are becoming more and more like men's. In the 1950s, twice as many men as women smoked. Today the numbers are even, and the real cause for concern is that teenaged girls are picking up the habit faster than boys. Traditionally men gorged themselves on bacon and eggs, ordered the big steak and baked potato dripping with butter, and stuffed themselves with desserts. Today some studies show the diet of the average woman contains marginally more saturated fat than that of the average man, and women, perhaps because they spend more time sitting behind desks than they used to, actually get less exercise than men.

Says Professor Kay-Tee Khaw, head of clinical gerontology at Cambridge University: "Over the past fifty years there has been a big rise in heart disease. It hit men first and has only affected women later because of a dramatic change in lifestyles among many women. Although death rates from heart disease in Britain are falling, the decline is slower among women than among men. In England between 1981 and 1991, heart disease death rates fell by only 17 percent in women compared with 25 percent in men."

If you talk about stress — another major risk factor for coronary heart disease — women are fast outstripping their male counterparts. Research shows that women in stressful jobs who have frequent fights at home were almost twice as likely to have heart attacks as women in jobs with less stress and a more peaceful home life. Women used to have time for friends, time for their children. Today many are frazzled wrecks as they try to hold down a full-time job while they're still expected to be supermom at home.

The Framingham study that followed ten thousand initially healthy subjects revealed that 35 percent of the heart attacks in women went unrecognized compared with 28 percent in men. In the United States nationally 48 percent of men who die of heart attacks have had no previous symptoms, but for women the figure is 63 percent. Even when they know something is wrong, heart attack symptoms in women can confuse them — and their doctors. Instead of the familiar pressure on the chest that men generally experience, the first sign of a heart attack in a woman may be a burning feeling in the neck or the shoulders. They may feel simply tired or nauseous — hardly the warning you expect from a life-threatening event. If they do make it to the hospital, the results of many of the diagnostic tests commonly used — like the treadmill exercise test — are less reliable for women. And too often women think advice on how to avoid coronary heart disease is not for them.

That's a mistake. The same risk factors that apply to men — heart disease in the family background, smoking, high blood cholesterol, low proportion of HDL cholesterol to LDL cholesterol, bad diet, and lack of exercise — apply equally to them. The Arizona Heart Institute has developed a set of tests for women to assess their heart risk. It takes in the common factors just mentioned, but also pinpoints some risks especially pertinent to women. Diabetes is often the forgotten indicator for heart disease, for instance, and it is just as potent a risk for women as for men. A woman who has gone through menopause or has had a hysterectomy at forty or earlier should be on the alert, especially if she is not taking an estrogen supplement. Age is also crucial, with the greatest danger occurring from fifty-one on.

It's all sound advice. But it misses one point. It's important, of course, for women now in the danger zone of life to take proper precautions. But there is real trouble ahead for a generation of teenagers and young women who, through smoking, lack of exercise, stress, and reliance on today's on-the-run, high-fat diets, will make today's death figures look in time positively rosy. They're the ones who need to hear the message.

HEART DISEASE:
WHAT YOU CAN DO ABOUT IT

What can you do about heart disease? Getting different parents might be a good start. Heredity plays a big part. If your father, mother, brother or sister, or even uncle or aunt died of heart disease, you are at serious risk. It's estimated that up to 66 percent of those having heart attacks under fifty-five had a family history of heart disease.

Okay, so you can't very easily change your parents. What can you change? If you smoke, giving up the puffs tops the list. High blood pressure — hypertension — is a huge and largely hidden risk. In North America it's estimated about one in four adults has elevated blood pressure and often fewer than half that number are getting treatment. Cutting your blood pressure level by about 3 percent — usually through diet and excercise and, if necessary, drugs — reduces your chances of coronary heart disease by 16 percent. High overall cholesterol totals are another major risk factor. As we saw earlier, it's the ratio between LDL and HDL that's important. A ratio of 5:1 is average, but 3:1 cuts heart attack risk by 50 percent. For every point you increase your HDL cholesterol, Dr. Meir Stamfer at Harvard University estimates the risk of heart disease is reduced by 7 percent.

Add high blood pressure and raised blood cholesterol, plus a lack of exercise, and you're probably looking at someone who is overweight — another indicator for coronary heart disease.

The best advice if you want to improve your survival chances is, first of all, have your doctor check your blood cholesterol level and blood pressure and explain the significance of the figures.

Second, get some exercise. Regular exercise should be part of our daily lives. A lot of us say we don't have time for exercise. What we're saying is, we don't have time to live. Try walking to work, or to the next station, cycling on errands instead of taking the car, finding a pool near work for that lunchtime swim.

Third, eat fresh fruits and vegetables. Improved diet is just as important — and often just as difficult to combine with busy lives. It's hard to avoid processed foods, but we can choose them more carefully for low fat content, and supplement them with those irreplaceable fresh fruits and vegetables.

Until quite recently, these were the three main approaches to reduce your risk for heart attack. Now another factor enters into the equation. Moderate consumption of alcohol, and especially wine, has joined the list of options.

CHAPTER III

Wining and Dining

THE WINE REVOLUTION

It was in Cardiff, Wales, that citadel of song and rugby football — but definitely not of wine — that the modern wine revolution had its beginnings. There, in 1978, a young scientist named Dr. A. Selwyn St. Leger, working for the epidemiological unit of the Medical Research Council, carried out a more or less random search for clues to the causes of coronary heart disease (CHD).

It began as another of those scientific fishing expeditions in which researchers throw a number of possible risk or benefit factors into the pot, give it a stir, and see what comes up. St. Leger and two colleagues were comparing CHD death rates in eighteen countries, including Canada, the United States, the United Kingdom, the Republic of Ireland, France, Italy, and Australia, with a whole batch of statistics covering everything from saturated fat intake to the availability of doctors. And they weren't really getting anywhere.

The availability of doctors or nurses didn't seem to have a bearing on the number of cardiac deaths, and total fat consumption as well as cigarette smoking, as expected, boosted CHD deaths. Alcohol consumption came in as a major protective element against the disease. But that was not entirely unexpected because the Klatsky study in Oakland, California, and the Honolulu study of Japanese men had already identified the U-shaped curve, in which moderate drinkers seem better protected against coronary heart disease than either abstainers or heavy drinkers.

And then luck knocked at the door. "It just so happened," St. Leger told me, "that by pure chance we were able to get hold of alcohol consumption by country, actually split into its components, beer, wine, and spirits." St. Leger and crew decided to break down that promising alcohol figure, just to see if any one type of beverage was better than any other. The results were astonishing.

When applied to CHD death rates for men, aged fifty-five to sixty-four (the highest risk period for males), it was clear that wine was more protective by a country mile. The figure below tells the story.

At the left, beer and spirits bastions like Finland, Scotland, the United States, New Zealand, Canada, England and Wales, Ireland, and Norway are way up there with the highest death rates from coronary heart disease. Down at the bottom of the slope, with the lowest rates of heart disease, are the wine-consuming countries, France, Italy, Switzerland, and Austria, with West Germany (as it then was) slipping under the wire too.

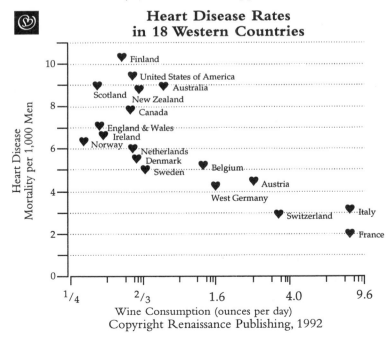

Heart Disease Rates
in 18 Western Countries

Wine Consumption (ounces per day)
Copyright Renaissance Publishing, 1992

The St. Leger team published their findings in *The Lancet* in May, 1979, and even today, reading between the lines, you can sense the excitement behind their professionally cautious conclusions. The wine finding was "by far the most interesting result to emerge." The connection was so profound that it was quite possible, they speculated that the whole protective benefit identified by Klatsky and others derived from wine and not from other alcoholic beverages. Their next words were prophetic. "If wine has a protective effect against [CHD] death, then this is, in view of our results, more likely to be due to constituents other than alcohol. Wines are rich in aromatic compounds and other trace components which give them their distinct character and it may be to these that we should look for the protective effect."

The next step, they proposed, should be research to determine the effects of wine on blood lipids and other blood constituents as well as platelet aggregation ("stickiness"). At the end, St. Leger could not resist adding a cry from the heart: "If wine is ever found to contain a constituent protective against [CHD] then we [would] consider it almost a sacrilege that this constituent should be isolated. The medicine is already in a highly palatable form, (as every connoisseur will confirm)."

St. Leger, years ahead of anyone else, had set the direction for research that could have a huge impact on saving lives. The paper caused a considerable stir when it was published, and St. Leger was in demand for media interviews. So what did he do next? He forgot it.

"The funny thing is that, after we'd done that work, I moved on to other things and rather forgot about it," he said in his delightful, slightly absent-minded manner. St. Leger, now forty-eight and a senior lecturer and consultant in public health at Manchester University, studied obscure subjects having to do with the organization of the National Health Service. No one was more astonished than he when he was invited in late 1994 to an international conference in Slovenia on the health aspects of wine where, he says, still incredulous, he was greeted "as a sort of guru."

"It's you!" exclaimed Elisabeth Holmgren, research director of the Wine Institute in San Francisco, on meeting him. "We thought you were dead or in your eighties! *You* started all this off."

What he started off was not so much a concerted research effort to identify possible health benefits from wine but rather a sort of pitter-patter of research, a project here, a project there, with the scientists often working in isolation and with little money. As mentioned, government research money in this area goes almost exclusively to projects related to the ill effects of alcohol, and not to research that might disturb that doomsday picture.

The next breakthrough came the year after the St. Leger results when two scientists at the Wistar Institute of Anatomy and Biology in Philadelphia, David Klurfeld and David Kritchevsky, conducted an animal experiment to compare the effects of wine, beer, and spirits in protecting against atherosclerosis. They devised a food regimen equivalent to the North American diet in all its fatty glory. This, plus doses of cholesterol, they fed to forty-eight male Dutch belted rabbits for three months. At the same time, the rabbits were divided into six groups, which were given respectively, water (the control group), ethanol (pure alcohol), red wine, white wine, beer, and whisky.

At the end of the three months, the animals were dispatched to bunny heaven while Klurfeld and Kritchevsky pored over their hearts and arteries. Sure enough, fatty foam cells — similar to the fatty streaks found in human arteries — were in evidence. The scientists, in fact, were surprised at the speed with which the North American-style diet had produced atherosclerosis in the rabbits.

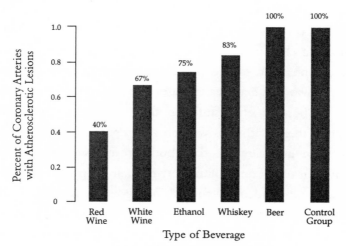

Atherosclerosis in Rabbits

Adapted from Klurfeld et al.,
Experimental and Molecular Pathology, 1990

But not in all rabbits to the same extent. One hundred percent of the rabbits in the control group had developed fatty lesions in their coronary arteries, as had those that drank beer. The rabbits on whisky had a score of 83 percent; ethanol, 75 percent; white wine, 67 percent; and red wine, way down at 40 percent. "Aortic atherosclerosis was reduced significantly by red wine," the authors concluded. "The biblical injunction, 'Drink no longer water, but use a little wine for thy stomach's sake' (1 Timothy 5:23), is supported by available scientific evidence." And like the first swallows in spring, patient studies were beginning to confirm that there was something special about wine.

Most of the population studies on alcohol and coronary heart disease up to 1980 had involved men fifty and older. They reflected the traditional and increasingly outdated medical prejudice that said women, especially those under fifty, were relatively immune to heart disease. In 1981 University of Boston Medical School researcher Lynn Rosenberg was about to shake that preconception.

Like so many studies in the alcohol field, this one began as something else entirely. In the course of a study on the impact of oral contraceptives on women, Rosenberg identified no fewer than 513 women between the ages of thirty and forty-nine who were in hospital after suffering their first heart attacks. She matched them with 918 women in hospital for other reasons, and nurse interviewers asked both groups detailed questions about their use of oral contraceptives, their weight, whether they smoked, and incidentally, their drinking habits. It was only after she had completed her contraceptive study that Rosenberg realized she also had invaluable information on the possible protective effects of alcohol — for once as it affected women.

She went back to her figures and discovered, not surprisingly considering what we now know about alcohol's protective potential, that nondrinkers were at greater risk for heart attacks than moderate drinkers. The preferred beverage among drinkers was spirits, followed by wine and then beer. But it turned out the wine drinkers had the greatest protection — they were a full 50 percent less likely to have a heart attack than women who didn't drink at all. Liquor drinkers had 10 percent protection, beer drinkers, 20 percent.

In Oakland, meanwhile, Dr. Arthur Klatsky was busy once again at his magic computer studying the patient records of 129,000 subjects and their drinking preferences. He, too, found that wine drinkers were at a significantly lower risk of heart attack than those who drank spirits or beer. This time white wine showed a slight advantage over red wine. The reason could be that, in California especially, white wine became the choice of millions in the 1980s for its "light" image and sweet taste. It was a wine that appealed to a new generation of sippers who had not accustomed themselves to the sharper taste and dense flavour of red wine. Klatsky warned that the figures showing wine ahead of beer and spirits needed "cautious interpretation." Wine drinkers, he said, tended to be wealthier and healthier than those drinking beer or spirits.

By 1986, Klatsky and his colleagues were reporting that the risk of being hospitalized for coronary heart disease was 11 percent lower for wine consumers than for beer or spirit drinkers. And in 1990 they reported that moderate consumers of wine had 50 percent less chance of dying of a heart attack than abstainers, and 20 percent less chance of dying of all causes. The equivalent figures for beer drinkers were 30 and 10 percent; for spirit drinkers, 40 percent and about the same risk of overall death as abstainers.

It was all rather frustrating. Here a hint, there a whisper that wine might be the best answer. The difficulty was that, although there had been scads of population studies showing that alcohol saved hearts, few of them separated out the different alcoholic beverages. And, where wine did come out tops, as in some of Dr. Klatsky's studies, there were always reservations or qualifications expressed.

In December 1994, I had met at a conference in Toronto Dr. Martin Grønbæk, a remarkably youthful-looking research fellow at the Danish Epidemiological Science Centre in Copenhagen. His group had followed the fates of six thousand men and seven thousand women between the ages of thirty and seventy-nine over a twelve-year period, carefully keeping tabs on their drinking and smoking habits and other factors. One of the most encouraging findings in a paper they had just published was that the women in the study derived just as much protection from similar amounts of alcohol as men. It suggested, Grønbæk told me, that the traditional advice that women should drink less should be reviewed.

Was there a difference depending on the type of drink consumed? Suddenly Grønbæk became mysterious. A paper would be published shortly on that subject; until then, he said, he could say nothing. During that winter I heard rumours that the Grønbæk study would plump for wine.

There were delays in publication. Then, on May 5, when their paper was published in the *British Medical Journal*, the story hit the headlines around the world. The Danish figures showed that nearly all the heart- and life-protective benefits came from drinking wine. The more wine you drank — up to a level of three to five glasses a day — the less risk you ran of dying of a heart attack or stroke. In fact, the less risk you ran of dying of any disease. The risk for heart attack or stroke at that level of consumption was cut by 60 percent, for all-cause mortality, by 50 percent. By comparison, those who drank three to five glasses of beer a day cut their heart attack or stroke risk by 30 percent, but experienced only a very slight reduction in their all-cause mortality risk.

The worst news was reserved for the chaps who make schnapps — Denmark's beloved fire in a glass — and for spirits distillers everywhere. This large study found a very slight benefit for those who only consumed spirits on a monthly basis. One to two drinks a day of spirits provided no more protection than abstaining would, while three to five drinks produced a one-third increase in the risk of heart attack, stroke, and all-cause mortality.

The surprise in the Danish study was not just that it was wine that made the difference, but the amount of wine. Five glasses equals approximately a bottle of wine a day. This goes far beyond the two, maybe three, glasses a day most experts recommend, and, many would argue, would take a lot of drinkers into the danger zone where the risks start to multiply. It should be remembered, though, that Sir Richard Doll, in his famous pronouncement in Sydney, stated that alcohol's protective effect was evident at up to four drinks a day — roughly in line with the Copenhagen finding.

Some were surprised that the result emerged from Denmark, which most of us would associate with schnapps and Carlsberg or Tuborg beer, but not with wine. The figures tell a different story. Next to the United Kingdom, Denmark has shown the biggest increase in wine consumption of any country, with consumption doubling in the last fifteen years. That may help to explain, suggest Grønbæk and his colleagues, why coronary heart disease declined by 30 percent in the same period. The authors speculate that the influence of Denmark's Common Market partners has helped to promote wine sales. Whatever the cause, Danes consume a surprising twenty-two litres of wine per head annually, much of it imported from the Bordeaux and Burgundy regions of France. (These two regions, as we shall see presently, produce red wines that are notable for their heart-protective qualities.)

The questions raised by the Danish study — about the superiority of wine to beer and spirits, and about the optimum amount to drink — will be debated by scientists for years to come. Undeniably, though, the study goes a long way towards explaining the French Paradox.

In the meantime we can echo the words of an editorial in the London *Times* published the day after the report was released: Grønbæk and colleagues "deserve to have their names cited with grand approval, and to have toasts of gratitude drunk to them across the land . . . To their use of a glass, and to what they pour in it, we say skol!"

THE FRENCH PARADOX

 The scene: a small restaurant in one of the southern suburbs of Lyon, in France.

The time: lunch hour.

Enter: A gentle, very Gallic professor, *Daily Telegraph* journalist in tow.

The proprietor, portly and expansive, describes the pleasures to come: unhung Scottish partridge, roasted in its own fat and bathed in champagne sauce, wild mushrooms, foie gras, and raw partridge liver. The meal begins with a salad of lettuce, apple, and cheese, served with crème fraiche dressing, and ends with cheese, coffee, and chocolate truffles. A bottle of the host's very best red Bordeaux provides the accompaniment.

It is a meal to make any modern nutritionist blanch. But not to worry: it's just Professor Serge Renaud doing the nutritional equivalent of walking on the waves to impress another foreign journalist. The truffles and the crème fraiche were a trifle on the excessive side, he allows, but the cheese, in spite of its sky-high calorie content, wouldn't do a bit of harm.

If he had more time from his work at the nearby laboratories of the French National Institute for Health and Medical Research (INSERM), Professor Renaud would have taken his guest another four hundred kilometres southwest to Toulouse for what some would regard as an even more startling gastronomic horror show. There, butcher's shops bulge with pickled corn-fed goose and duck, entombed in waxy white fat, while goose hearts, sausages, every sort of foie gras, and, of course, a huge variety of cheeses make up the daily fare.

You would expect that the southern France diet, plus the fact that the French generally seem to be puffing on Galois cigarettes and shunning any form of physical activity, provides booming business for local coronary care units. And you'd be wrong. The people of Toulouse have one of the lowest rates of coronary artery disease in the world. A male living in Stanford, California, is more than twice as likely to have a heart attack than a man in Toulouse; a male living in Halifax, Nova Scotia, is nearly three times as likely to have a heart attack as his opposite number in Toulouse.

Professor Renaud, an epidemiologist who spent a good part of his medical career in Canada, believes the French get off lightly partly due to the local diet, which, he says, isn't nearly as bad for the system as you'd expect. Goose and duck fat, he believes, are simply not as damaging as the saturated fats used in more northerly countries. But a good part of the credit for the spectacularly low heart attack rate, he believes, goes to alcohol. And when we're talking about alcohol in Toulouse, we're talking about red wine.

Renaud, the prophet of what is now known as the French Paradox, first came to international attention on that now-famous *60 Minutes* broadcast in November 1991. The item opened innocuously enough with correspondent Morley Safer pondering why it was that the French, who eat 30 percent more fat than Americans, and smoke more and exercise less, suffer fewer heart attacks. "If you're a middle-aged American man, your chances of dying of a heart attack are three times greater than a Frenchman of the same age," he said. "So it's obvious the French are doing something right, something Americans are not doing."

Safer made the inevitable excursion to a restaurant in Lyon, hesitating over a menu that featured pig's head pâté, black pudding, potatoes in oil, dishes drenched in butter and cream, and rounded off with healthy servings of oh-so-fatty cheese. How could the French defy rules of nutrition that seem immutable everywhere else in the world?

"Well," suggested his luncheon companion, Professor Renaud, "my explanation is, of course, the consumption of alcohol." Many doctors, said Safer in voice-over, believe that alcohol, and particularly red wine, reduces the risk of heart disease. "Now that is all but confirmed." Moderate alcohol consumption reduces coronary heart disease by as much as 50 percent, said Renaud. What did he mean by moderate? asked Safer. "I mean a few glasses of wine per day. If you're just sticking to that, you will never get drunk."

A number of American doctors, said Safer, had told him if it was up to them, they would get rid of milk in school lunchrooms and exchange it for watered wine. "The [North] American milk habit, they said, is priming our twelve-year-olds for heart attacks at fifty." Safer, sipping a glass of wine, pointed out that while the United States is among the lowest consumers of wine in the world (seven litres per capita compared with nine in Canada, twelve in the United Kingdom, and sixty-seven in France), it has one of the highest heart attack rates. And the one section of the country that consumes the least wine — the so-called "Bible Belt" in southern United States — is referred to by doctors as "Stroke Alley."

And that was it. By the next day, Americans and Canadians were on the way to their wine shops in droves. The *Wall Street Journal* reported that in the four weeks following the broadcast, sales of Cabernet Sauvignon sales went up 45 percent. The Robert Mondavi winery in California announced its Cabernet sales were up 50 percent. When the show was rebroadcast during the summer re-run period, the rush began all over again. Red wine sales (from an admittedly low base) have remained at 15 percent above previous levels since (even though total wine consumption in the United States has declined in recent years).

Similar increases were noted in wine sales in Canada.

Doctors had been aware for decades that French CHD mortality figures were inexplicably low — especially in view of the high-fat French diet. Some simply put it down to sloppy French medical practices, suggesting that often "sudden death" was filled in as the cause of death when a more careful examination would have resulted in a diagnosis of coronary heart disease. Many believed this theory and dismissed the French Paradox as a fraud. Also, as in so many other areas of life, fashion plays a part in medicine. Coronary heart disease as a commonly reported cause of death caught on early in the century in the United States, and spread to Britain by the 1930s. Perhaps the French, so fashionable in many other regards, had simply not caught up with this "fashion." And then Monica arrived.

Monica was no Florence Nightingale of the coronary wards: "she" was a ten-year study initiated by the World Health Organization and designed to put an end once and for all to quibbling over international CHD comparisons. At a 1978 international conference on coronary heart disease in Bethesda, Maryland, general dissatisfaction was expressed at the unreliability of coronary mortality rates from different countries. Only when these were ironed out, argued the scientists, would it be possible to get a handle on what was really causing the huge variations from country to country. Monica would be the answer.

Forty-one cities around the world, most of them in Europe, were selected for the study. Starting in 1985, meticulous records would be kept of fatal and nonfatal heart attacks in those communities. Every effort would be made to ensure that the statistics were gathered in a uniform manner so that valid comparisons could be made. In Canada, Halifax was selected; in the United States, Stanford, California; in the United Kingdom,

Glasgow and Belfast; in Australia, Newcastle and Perth; in New Zealand, Auckland; and in France, Lille, Strasbourg, and Toulouse.

When the Monica team, headed by Dr. Hugh Tunstall-Pedoe of the University of Dundee, issued its report in 1994, the disparities were startling. Women in Glasgow, for example, were more than eight times as likely to die of a heart attack as women in Catalonia, Spain. For men, North Karelia in Finland pipped Glasgow at the post for the very worst mortality rate from coronary heart disease, while Beijing had the best (although many speculate that, down the road, there will be a price to pay for the huge increase in smoking in China in recent years). The disparity: men in North Karelia were twelve times as likely to have a heart attack as men in Beijing.

Of course, the French results were the ones awaited with the greatest eagerness. It would not be surprising if countries enjoying low-fat diets, like Spain and Italy, came up with good results. But the French, with their pâtés and cheeses, were doing it all wrong. Yet there were the figures: among men the heart attack rates in Lille and Strasbourg were a very respectable 314 and 336 per 100,000, respectively. Toulouse, in the southwest, did even better at 240. And Catalonia, Spain, was better still at 187, while the men of Friuli, in northern Italy, turned in a respectable 270. Confirming St. Leger's findings of fifteen years earlier, the wine-consuming countries seemed to come off best — Spain, Italy, and even Switzerland (Vaud/Fribourg scored a low 253). If wine was one of the major factors, then it seemed even powerful enough to overcome the excesses of the French diet and lifestyle.

In contrast with the sunny south, the figures for males in northern Europe were dismal. Glasgow clocked in at a horrendous 823, Belfast at 781. Finnish men took the dubious title for most prone to heart disease, their three study centres scoring 915, 824, and 593. The old Commonwealth countries did little better with Halifax scoring 605 (fifth worst for men, eighth for women), Auckland, 466, and the two Australian study centres, Newcastle and Perth, 561 and 422, respectively.

Everywhere women fared better than men. The redoubtable women of Toulouse came in with a heart attack rate of only 37 per 100,000, equalling the figure for Beijing women. In Halifax and Stanford, in comparison, women were nearly four times as likely to have heart attacks as those in Toulouse and Beijing.

Monica had done her job. The French Paradox had been confirmed. Now the big job was to figure out exactly why people in Mediterranean countries — and southern France in particular — enjoyed this huge health advantage.

Professor Renaud hadn't waited for the final report. Using preliminary Monica figures, he had already published a paper in *The Lancet* in 1992 that, while properly cautious, had hinted that red wine was largely responsible for the favourable Toulouse figures. A 1991 study in which he had been an adviser in Caerphilly, Wales, had shown that the platelets, so important in causing life-threatening clots, had shown much less tendency to clump together with moderate alcohol consumption. Other studies in Scotland and France had shown that alcohol seemed to work better in France in reducing the stickiness of the platelets — a finding that might be related to wine consumption in France.

"The high wine intake and low mortality from [coronary heart disease] in Toulouse may be considered surprising," Renaud wrote, tongue just slightly in cheek. "Nevertheless, this observation accords with previous reports [principally, St. Leger's] of an inverse association between consumption of alcohol and cardiac mortality in developed countries, the potentially beneficial effect of alcohol being reported as essentially due to consumption of wine."

There simply didn't seem to be anything else that could account for the French Paradox, Renaud argued. Cholesterol levels in Toulouse were almost identical to those in Belfast, moderately lower than those in Glasgow, but actually higher than those in Stanford, California, where the heart attack risk was double that in the French city. Systolic blood pressure, again a good indicator for coronary heart disease, was only slightly lower in Toulouse than in Glasgow and Belfast, and slightly higher than the figure for Stanford.

Only in terms of the percentage of cigarette smokers did Toulouse enjoy a clear advantage over Glasgow. In the Scottish city, notorious for its high tobacco consumption, half the men and women smoke (by contrast, in Toulouse, 37 percent of men and only 17 percent of women smoke). The proportion of men smoking in Belfast (34 percent) is actually lower than the Toulouse figure, although 33 percent of women smoke in the Northern Ireland community. There didn't seem to be any answers there.

Apart from wine consumption, the only other factor that seemed to correlate with coronary heart disease was consumption of dairy fat, with butter and milk-slurping countries like the United States, Canada, Finland, and the United Kingdom coming off poorly in the CHD figures. But France — and Switzerland too — defied the dairy fat argument. The French and the Swiss love their cheeses, and consume them massively, yet both have low CHD rates. Renaud has since theorized that in cheese form, dairy fat may not be as harmful. In his 1992 paper he prognosticated that in France and Switzerland, "the untoward effects of saturated fats are counteracted by intake of wine."

Why did wine work better than, say, the vodka the Finns drink, or Scottish pints? Renaud speculated that apart from any inherent properties of wine, it might be that because wine is mostly consumed during meals, it hits the system at the optimum time — when unsaturated fats from the meal are putting the body at maximum stress. And, because it is absorbed slowly, its protective effect lasts longer. The other ingredients of the French Paradox, according to Boston cardiologist Dr. Curtis Ellison, are:

(The French appetite for fresh fruit and vegetables, the latter eaten raw or cooked only lightly.

(More relaxed, drawn-out meals — and no snacks in between meals.

(A different fat protocol that involves leaner meat, smaller meat portions, dairy fat in the form of cheese rather than milk, and the use of olive oil or goose fat in cooking. The theory is that fats used in these forms are less harmful.

Ellison adds: "Red wine seems to have special protective properties. There are lots of tantalizing possibilities with red wine, but all the data are not in yet."

Renaud's French Paradox and its likely connection to wine have teased and provoked scientists. They keep coming back to it, like dogs to an old bone, gnawing it, tossing it in the air, looking for the meat they may have missed the first time. Take the headline in the London *Daily Telegraph* on September 13, 1994: "Diet: a myth exposed, a secret revealed. Scientists debunk red wine theory on heart disease."

The article quoted Professor Tunstall-Pedoe, coordinator of the Monica study, as saying, "It is not a French Paradox and the French are not a model for the rest of the world to follow." Part of the reason for low cardiac mortality figures in France, he explained, reviving the old saw about French inefficiency, was that heart attack deaths were frequently labelled "sudden death," giving a false impression that the coronary death rate was low.

But the whole point of the Monica study, of course, was that it also recognized nonfatal heart attacks — where there was little chance of misdiagnosis. And the French, even allowing for a slight adjustment for "sudden death" diagnoses, still come out close to the bottom for heart attack risk — even though they eat more fat, smoke more, and exercise less than most of their neighbours.

Monica did indeed "validate that these differences in mortality are real," Tunstall-Pedoe told me when I called on him at Ninewells Hospital, in Dundee. "It really is true that there is five or ten times as much coronary disease in some populations as there is in others." If you shave a bit off the French figures to allow for misdiagnosis on death certificates, the French are still near the bottom of the table along with other Mediterranean countries like Spain and Italy. "It's more a case of the Mediterranean Paradox than the French Paradox," he said. And the article in the *Telegraph*? "Newspapers have to sensationalize things," he said defensively.

The professor, to be polite, was talking through his hat. French heart attack rates are amongst the lowest in the world. And the paradox lies in the fact that, unlike Spain, Italy, or even Japan — all countries with low rates — the French consume an inordinate amount of saturated fats. They have no business being near the bottom of the table. But they are. The paradox stands. And the real question is, how much does the hefty French appetite for alcohol, and wine in particular, contribute to that anomaly?

When I finally met Serge Renaud in December 1994, at a

conference in Toronto, he was feeling tired and a little battered. His stand on the French Paradox had attracted enormous attention and put him under a good deal of pressure. He has always been reasonably cautious about his claims for wine ("it is not my job to tell people what to drink," he says), but his theories have come under attack nevertheless.

Renaud was feeling especially sore about Tunstall-Pedoe's remarks. "I don't know what happened to him to say that," he said. Tunstall-Pedoe's own figures showed that French rates for nonfatal heart attacks — about which there can be no doubt because they have been properly diagnosed in hospital — confirm that French CHD rates are among the lowest in the world. However, he had only words of praise for St. Leger, whom he had only recently met for the first time. "I used his study to go a step further for the French Paradox," he said.

The connection between wine consumption and coronary heart disease had only strengthened in the most recent studies, he continued. He estimates that wine provides 30 to 40 percent more protection against coronary heart disease than beer or spirits. "All the countries that drink a lot of wine, they are protected," said Renaud. "We can't argue with that." He predicted that studies now underway will finally determine how much of the French Paradox is due to wine and how much to dietary and other factors.

There were still, said Renaud, far too many people overindulging in alcohol in France, leading to high cirrhosis and cancer death rates, as well as high rates of suicide and traffic deaths. "We still have a large number of people drinking more than a litre of wine per day," he said. "And I would guess some of them are more than two litres. But two or three glasses of wine per day — perfect! If everyone would drink that in France there would be very few accidents [due to alcohol], very few cancers, and much longer life expectancy."

Professor Renaud was sixty-seven at the time and looking forward to retiring in 1996 to his little seaside house near Bordeaux. The sparkle came back to his eye when I asked him to describe to me the kind of meal he enjoys when in that southwest corner of France. "It should be starting with goose lee-ver," he said. "Fresh goose lee-ver. Just cooked a leetle beet. And duck. Pieces of duck. How audacious it is, the duck! And fruit — only fruit — for dessert. And, of course, a good bottle of Medoc!"

NOT BY WINE ALONE: THE MEDITERRANEAN DIET

After concluding that red wine was indeed protective against coronary heart disease, Dr. Serge Renaud now set out to discover just how important the Mediterranean diet was in preserving lives. He could hardly have conceived of a more rigorous test. His team focused on six hundred male patients at the Lyon Cardiovascular Hospital, all of whom had experienced a first heart attack. The patients were divided into two groups. Half (the control group) were put on the normal low-fat diet prescribed for heart patients the world over. The other half (the experimental group) were put on a Mediterranean-style diet that included more bread, more root vegetables and green vegetables, more fish, and less meat (with red meats being replaced by poultry). Interestingly, because the patients were from the centre of France, and were not as accustomed to heavy use of olive oil as their compatriots further south, the research team developed a canola oil margarine for the experimental group to take the place of cream and butter. Some olive oil was still used for cooking and salads.

Both groups were allowed moderate amounts of cheese and wine (depriving any group of French people of these two essentials of life, even in the name of science, would have been considered a blow too cruel). After twenty-seven months Renaud and his team ran into a major snag. "The experiment had to be stopped," Renaud told me in Toronto. "It would have been unethical to continue." The reason: too many of the patients on the regular diet were dying compared with those on the Mediterranean diet.

"You cannot continue," said Renaud. "You are watching them die." The chances of patients on the Mediterranean diet having a second heart attack or experiencing sudden death were 70 percent less than those on the regular diet. The reduction in all-cause mortality in the experimental group was even better — between 70 and 80 percent. The results, said Dr. Renaud, could have been even better. Although patients in the experimental group were advised to drink moderate amounts of wine with their food, one-third didn't. Of the three who died from cardiac causes in the experimental group (compared with sixteen in the control group), none was a wine drinker. The astonishing thing was that risk factors like blood pressure, LDL cholesterol levels, and weight levels followed a similar and slowly decreasing pattern in both groups (there were slightly more smokers in the Mediterranean diet group).

The only significant difference was that after a year, the Mediterranean diet group had significantly higher antioxidant levels (about which we'll learn more later) in their blood. Renaud's experiment had helped show that the relative invulnerability of people in the Mediterranean areas of Europe to coronary heart disease apparently has as much to do with food as it does with wine. The message was clear: to get maximum protection, conventional low-fat diets are not enough. It takes, in addition to regular modest consumption of the right wines, a wholesale switch to the kind of foods people eat on the shores of the Mediterranean.

This was not news to people at the Boston head office of one of the oddest public interest health groups around: the Oldways Preservation and Exchange Trust. It's not like any health organization you've ever heard of. Where most citizen health groups are concerned with disease — finding a cure for cancer, heart disease, or Parkinson's disease, whatever ails us — Oldways wants to keep us well. Its concern is seeing we don't get those diseases in the first place. And its founders are convinced that many of the important answers lie with the ancient diets of the human race as opposed to today's supermarket techno-junk food. Oldways has been promoting the idea of the Mediterranean diet for several years as the solution to many of our diet-induced illnesses.

The idea for Oldways grew out of a trip Boston lawyer K. Dun Gifford took to China in 1987. He was shocked to discover that, during the Cultural Revolution, the Red Guards had destroyed much of China's culinary heritage, burning ancient cookery books and expelling or killing the people who were the modern repositories of the Chinese cuisine. Gifford realized that, what the Red Guards had done in China, the huge multinational food companies were doing elsewhere in the world, persuading people to give up their "peasant" diets in favour of pre-packaged dinners and fast-food hamburgers.

With his children grown up, Gifford was looking for a new purpose in life. He returned to Boston with the Oldways idea in his head. "I really intended it to be a sort of archive, sending people around the world to record the information on food before it was lost," he said. But Oldways's timing was brilliant. It arrived on the scene just when many Westerners were looking for alternative answers to the chemical junk diet being imposed on them by the food multinationals. Instead of being a mouse squeaking in the corner, Oldways found itself with a resounding voice in the international food debate.

The Mediterranean diet was a natural place to start (although Oldways has also started promoting the North African diet, and will launch a major effort on Asian diets late in 1995). Most people were already familiar to some extent with Italian, Greek, and southern French cooking, so it wasn't a great leap into the unknown. A conference on the Mediterranean diet in San Francisco in 1994 had a remarkable spillover effect. Restaurants started springing up dedicated to Mediterranean diet principles, magazines ran features about it, and it wasn't long before newspaper food editors in Canada, the United States, and Europe were telling their readers how to start reaping the heart benefits of the Mediterranean diet for their families. The Italian government, concerned about the inroads made by U.S. fast-food chains, has even asked Oldways to put on a conference in Italy on the virtues of traditional Italian food.

The diet's health benefits were nothing new. Studies as long ago as the 1950s had shown the people of Greece, especially of Crete, lived longer and enjoyed a much lower rate of cardiovascular disease and cancer when compared with almost anywhere else in the world. And olive oil seemed to be an important factor. The Cretans in the 1950s derived a surprisingly high 40 percent of their energy from fat, most of that in the form of olive oil. We now know that olive oil boosts the "good" HDL cholesterol and reduces the "bad" LDL cholesterol, as well as being high in vitamin E, which helps prevent hardening of the arteries. The argument for olive oil became even stronger in early 1995 when researchers at Harvard reported that, in a study of 820 Greek women with breast cancer and 1,548 healthy women, those who consumed olive oil more than once a day reduced their chances of getting breast cancer by 25 percent.

So what exactly is the Mediterranean diet? There is no single answer. The people of that part of the world have invented a thousand different variations on the healthy food theme. But there are common themes. Grain foods, like rice or pasta, should occupy the centre of the plate, says Gifford, with meat or fish to the side, almost as a sauce or seasoning. Garlic is important, and so is olive oil, either for cooking or for salads, or for brushing onto bread in place of butter or margarine. Fish, glorious fish — the anchovies, mackerel, herring, and sardines high in fish oils, as well as the blander, large, deep-sea specimens — hold place of honour. Deep frying is out, while oven broiling, with just a drizzle of oil, is in. The microwave comes into its own for cooking vegetables al dente, without dissipating any of the goodness.

In addition, says Gifford, don't dispense with all those rich cheeses because of their fat content; instead, use just tiny portions to give a flavour highlight. And if there's one word that typifies shopping and eating from Madrid to Athens, it's freshness. Buy the freshest fish, salad greens, fruit, and vegetables you can get your hands on. People tested in Toulouse had exceptionally high levels of vitamin C, which is also good for boosting HDL cholesterol. By contrast, people in Northern Ireland showed such low levels — presumably because of the lack of fruits and vegetables in the diet — that some were at risk of scurvy. "Oh, I made my husband a lovely salad," an Irish housewife was supposed to have told a researcher. "Was that last year, Joe, or the year before?"

The Traditional Healthy
Mediterranean Diet Pyramid

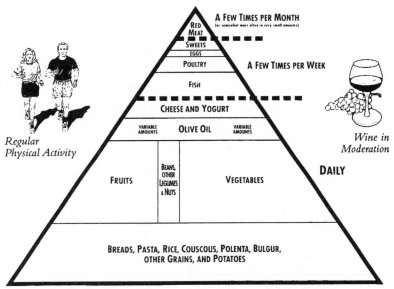

A FEW TIMES PER MONTH (or somewhat more often in very small amounts)

RED MEAT

SWEETS

EGGS

POULTRY

A FEW TIMES PER WEEK

FISH

CHEESE AND YOGURT

VARIABLE AMOUNTS · OLIVE OIL · VARIABLE AMOUNTS

Regular Physical Activity

Wine in Moderation

FRUITS

BEANS, OTHER LEGUMES & NUTS

VEGETABLES

DAILY

BREADS, PASTA, RICE, COUSCOUS, POLENTA, BULGUR, OTHER GRAINS, AND POTATOES

It's not only what you eat but how you eat it that counts. Mediterranean people, for instance, are not big snackers. They confine their eating to mealtimes — and such meals! The midday meal, of course, is the big production — a leisurely hour or two spent consuming several courses. And some studies have even suggested that the inevitable siesta that follows contributes to the overall protective effect that keeps coronary heart disease figures low.

How does the Mediterranean diet differ from the official diet line of most governments? It's instructive to compare two nutritional pyramids cardiologist Dr. Arthur Klatsky keeps on the wall of his Oakland, California, office to help his patients eat their way back to health and strength. One, the official U.S. Department of Agriculture's dietary recommendations, is "for people who simply like to be told not to eat this or that," says Klatsky. The other, Oldways's Mediterranean Diet Pyramid, takes another approach.

The first thing you notice in the Oldways version is that red meat has been relegated to the tiny apex of the pyramid. People are advised to eat it only a few times a month, or somewhat more often if used sparingly. On the government chart, because the U.S. government is under powerful pressure from beef (and dairy) producers, the meat issue is completely fudged. Meat, fish, beans, eggs, nuts, and dairy products are all lumped together and Americans are advised to eat two to three servings of them a day.

What on earth does that mean? Two servings of cashew nuts and a chickpea salad? Of course, for many Americans, it's simply an invitation to continue eating hamburgers, steaks, hot dogs, eggs, cheese, milk, and their other traditional staples while ignoring fish and legumes, which are regarded mostly with abhorrence and loathing. While fats and oils are, quite rightly, downplayed by the government nutritionists, on the Oldways pyramid, olive oil gets a prominent mention, and cheese and yogurt are approved for consumption a few times a week.

Come down to the bottom of the pyramid and you find the two groups largely in agreement in recommending frequent portions of fresh fruits and vegetables. Not too different also is the Agriculture Department's recommendation for hefty servings of bread, cereal, rice, and pasta, compared with the Oldways formula: breads, pasta, couscous (a North African semolina-like dish often served with meat sauce), polenta, bulgur (a Middle East cereal), other grains, and potatoes.

In 1994 the British government's Committee on the Medical Aspects of Food Policy (COMA) also recommended a diet that leaned more heavily on fruit, vegetables, bread and potatoes, and (ugh) steamed fish, and showed the door to heavy meat intake and the traditional British affection for cakes and sweets. But of olive oil and couscous, not a peep was heard from the British committee. And maybe that isn't surprising. The Mediterranean diet is largely plant-based. It isn't quite vegetarian, but it's not far from it. The British — and Canadians and Americans too — are not, on the whole, inclined to give up their preference for meat 'n' potatoes yet. And although in fashionable restaurants these days, the waiter pours olive oil on your plate for you to dip your roll in instead of spreading butter, olive oil is still not the popular choice of the average shopper.

Many people wouldn't even notice the most controversial item of all on the Oldways poster. To one side is a bunch of grapes and a wine glass together with an optional recommendation to enjoy a glass or two of wine a day. It's controversial because the pyramid was developed for Oldways by nutritionists from the Harvard School of Public Health and the European regional office of the World Health Organization (WHO). WHO, under the thrall of the temperance movement mainly in Scandinavia, has been adamant in trying to deny any possible health benefits related to the moderate consumption of alcohol. That little glass beside the pyramid was an important concession.

"People at WHO," said Greg Dresher, one of the founders of Oldways, "said it would be intellectually dishonest not to put in a glass of wine beside the pyramid. The advantages of mealtime wine are well-accepted in the public health community." That didn't stop a whole range of temperance and quasi-government addiction groups protesting the WHO endorsement of moderate wine consumption.

Olive oil, too, is not without its critics. Dr. Klatsky is

concerned that, because of its generous applications, fats total 35 percent of the energy intake in the Mediterranean diet, compared with 25 percent in the Department of Agriculture pyramid. It might not be the best answer for someone with a weight problem, he suggests. Like other doctors, he worries that people in the United States, Britain, Canada, and elsewhere might simply take to olive oil — without reducing their consumption of butter and other saturated fats. The effects could be unfortunate.

Also, he adds, some people just don't like the taste of olive oil. The answer might be canola (rapeseed) oil, a vegetable oil that is now used widely in margarine (and used in Renaud's hospital experiment) and that has been steadily gaining the approval of more and more nutritionists.

Is the Mediterranean diet practical for our "rush-rush" society? Even in Mediterranean countries the traditional diet is becoming less common as people adapt to a nine-to-five schedule, and women, juggling job and family responsibilities, have less time to cook those great meals. So what's the point? I asked Dun Gifford. What good does it do people today in Boston or Montreal or Bristol to know that some forty years ago people on the island of Crete had a simply marvellous diet?

"Hey, look at smoking!" he replied. A couple of decades ago the smoking problem seemed intractable. Today, with the exception of teenaged girls, smoking is on the decline in most developed countries. The irony is, said Gifford, that the enemy hasn't changed: the tobacco firms, concerned about their shrinking cigarette market, are now big operators in the mass-manufacture of food.

"Already," he pointed out, "restaurants are changing their menus." Restaurants in California are leading the way as far as the Mediterranean diet is concerned. Joyce Goldstein's Square One eatery in San Francisco boasts of serving only the freshest of fresh fruit and vegetables and couscous dishes you'd expect to eat beside the blue Mediterranean rather than the Pacific. Don't be surprised to see the same formula applied in your city or town. Supermarkets, too, are adapting, said Gifford. It's just as easy, after all, to make a profit selling foods that are healthful — fruits and salads, prepared legumes, and so on — as it is to get rich selling hot dogs and cream cakes.

LEARNING CONTINENTAL WAYS

In North America, the lessons of the healthful Mediterranean style of eating, and especially drinking, are slowly being learned. Too slowly, some would say. A few figures tell the story.

In the United States, wine consumption more than doubled between 1950 and 1990 — from 3.4 litres per head to 7.8 litres. There was an even more dramatic increase in Canada, where per capita consumption of wine increased fivefold in the same period to nearly 9 litres per capita in 1990. Compared with the table below, showing the countries where the most wine is consumed, Canada and the United States are still in the minor leagues.

But we are becoming classier about the way we drink. North America, unfortunately, opted in its earlier history for the northern European style of drinking, in which excessive amounts of booze were ingested with the single idea of becoming intoxicated. I saw the flagrant North American hypocrisy over alcohol at work when I arrived in Winnipeg as a young immigrant in 1958. Western Canada, like much of the mid-western and southern United States, was still firmly in the grip of the prohibitionists. Bars had only just begun to appear

Per Capita Consumption (L/year)

Country	1992		1991		1990		1989		1988	
France............	64.50	1	67.00	1	72.70	1	73.60	1	74.00	1
Luxemburg........	59.70	2	60.30	3	58.20	3	61.40	3	58.30	3
Portugal..........	55.00	3	62.00	2	50.00	5	53.00	5	54.00	5
Italy..............	—		60.28	4	61.45	2	71.56	2	72.10	2
Argentina.........	51.63	4	55.01	5	52.10	4	55.89	4	55.89	4
Switzerland........	44.47	5	47.20	6	47.41	6	47.74	6	48.17	6
Spain..............	39.10	6	39.77	8	41.97	7	41.97	7	45.85	7
Slovenia..........	39.00	7	40.00	7	—		—		—	
Austria............	33.10	8	33.70	9	35.00	8	35.00	9	33.90	10
Greece	31.50	9	32.40	10	—		—		—	
Hungary...........	30.00	10	30.00	11	—		—		—	
Chile.............	29.50	11	29.50	12	29.50	9	39.50	8	35.00	9
Denmark..........	25.56	12	23.60	15	—		—		—	
Uruguay..........	25.40	13	25.40	14	—		—		—	
Germany..........	22.80	14	26.10	13	—		—		—	
Roumania	21.30	15	19.30	16	26.00	10	17.00	10	42.80	8

Source: *Bulletin de l'O.I.V.* 1993, 753–754
O.I.V. Documentation

in sinful Toronto, but in most of the country, the only places you could buy a drink was in depressing beer parlours restricted mostly to men. In Winnipeg I was quickly introduced to the primitive custom of buying a bottle of rum on the way to a party — and passing it from person to person in the car to consume it as fast as possible before the police stopped you (you were only allowed to drive directly home with a bottle, without opening it).

Those dark ages are happily gone. There is almost a European sophistication about drinking today in most parts of North America, and that's largely due to the trend towards drinking wine. The bad news is that wine consumption, like the consumption of beer and liquor, is on the decline. In Canada, per capita wine consumption hit a peak of 10.31 litres in 1987, and has been waning since. Almost exactly the same drinking pattern is apparent in the United States — except that there wine consumption peaked in 1986 and has been on an even steeper decline ever since. (Alcohol consumption in the United States, in fact, is in its longest period of decline since Prohibition in the 1920s.)

In 1993, the latest year for which figures are available, wine consumption in the United States took another dramatic 6.7 percent drop while in Canada consumption dropped in 1994 by 3.6 percent. I'm not here to shed tears for the wine industry, but to express regret for an opportunity missed. All those years that wine consumption was climbing steadily, Americans and Canadians were growing to appreciate that wine could be consumed differently from the more traditional beer and spirits. It could be consumed with food, it was a more sociable drink, and there were less likely to be unfortunate aftereffects. They also demonstrated increasing sophistication as their tastes in wine expanded. And now we know wine drinkers were also doing their hearts a big favour.

So what went wrong? Why has wine consumption declined? There are some good reasons. Drinking and driving became less and less acceptable in North America, and so people cut back their consumption of all alcoholic beverages. And there are bad reasons: in this health-conscious age, a lot of people got the mistaken idea that any alcoholic beverage was fattening and generally bad for their health. On the contrary, alcohol in moderation is not fattening and is, as we have seen, one of the best things you can take to protect against coronary heart disease and other diseases.

There have also been deliberate scare campaigns to convince people that even light drinking could result in cancer or birth deformities. Another reason for the decline, as the Canadian drinks industry in particular points out, is that the dramatic increase in taxes on alcohol — generally unopposed because of the widespread conviction that booze is sinful — has helped to discourage consumption.

The Canadian and American experiences are in direct contrast to that of Britain, which continues to be one of the few countries in the world where wine consumption is increasing. The irony is that just at a time when wine consumption is dropping significantly in France (although they are still by far the world's largest consumers), the British have been taking to wine like . . . well . . . the French. On their way to becoming the most civilized — and potentially healthful — drinkers in the world, the British are providing an example that North Americans could usefully follow. No longer is the cozy British pub the place where nearly all the drinking is done. More and more, people are buying wine, usually in their local supermarket, and taking it home to drink. The result is fewer tipplers behind the wheel, and drink consumed in a more healthful fashion with food.

The switch to wine cuts right across class lines: from being an "upper-classy," wine-and-candlelight sort of thing, it's now the norm for the British to order a bottle of Sauterne or Riesling whenever they go into one of their ubiquitous curry houses.

In sex terms, too, there has been a change in drinking habits in North America, as well as Britain. Wine was always considered more of a "woman's drink," while men opted for beer. Surveys show more men are switching to wine, with, according to a British survey, men twice as likely as women to choose red wine over white. The big losers on both sides of the Atlantic have been the fortified wines — sherry and port — which have fallen prey to calorie concerns.

In Canada and the United States, the news for wine producers has not been all bad. While consumption has declined in recent years, people are buying better wines and paying more for them. Wine-tasting at vineyards in the Niagara Peninsula, California, and elsewhere has become a major tourist activity, exposing potential customers to a whole new generation of superior local wines.

Wine tours are all the rage in France, too, but they have done nothing to halt a major historical decline in French wine consumption. In 1990 the per capita wine consumption in France was only half what it had been in 1955. Many French people, of course, simply drank too much and paid a terrible price for it. The decline in alcohol abuse is the good news. The bad news is that younger French people are turning away from wine, just as they are turning away from the traditional French diet in favour of North American — style "berr-ger and cheeps." Although French heart attack rates are still almost the lowest in the world, they can be expected to change as the new diets and drinking habits take hold.

The bigger misfortune is already happening in the United States: more and more older Americans are becoming abstainers just at the very time in life when moderate alcohol consumption could most benefit them. Where 93 percent of men and 88 percent of women in the United Kingdom drink, in the United States the corresponding figures are 64 percent and 51 percent. Canada falls in between with 82 percent of men and 73 percent of women listing themselves as current or occasional drinkers.

The drinking pattern in Australia is similar, with 87 percent of men and 75 percent of women reporting in a Heart Foundation survey in 1989 that they drank, the overwhelming majority reporting that they had two drinks a day or less. But forget about those commercials with hearty Aussies on the beach quaffing Fosters; beer (as well as spirit) consumption has been in severe decline since 1975. For a while wine sales took up the slack, but in the last few years, while the rest of the world was discovering the glories of the better Australian wines, the Aussies were actually turning their backs on the stuff. Again, campaigns against drinking and driving have played an important part in reducing consumption and, like the Americans, more and more Australians are becoming abstainers — probably in the mistaken belief that they are improving their health.

In view of the new discoveries about wine's life-saving potential, the decline in consumption in Australia as well as Canada and the United States is more than a shame — it's a tragedy. Fortunately, it's a situation that could easily be remedied. As people become more aware of the protection wine (and, to a lesser degree, other alcoholic beverages) provide against heart disease, expect to see a swing in consumption patterns.

It won't mean a return to the bad old North American drinking pattern, with people skulking around clutching bottles in brown paper bags like criminals or concealing themselves from the light of day in dark, grungy beer parlours. This time, I predict, we'll see wine available in every sort of restaurant and cafeteria. Wine will become an accepted part of the dinnertime routine in more and more Canadian and American homes. And just as today wine lovers discuss aroma and flavour, tomorrow a new word will join the lexicon of wine appreciation: antioxidants.

CHAPTER IV

Uncorking Wine's Secrets

THE SURPRISING POWER OF ANTIOXIDANTS

What is it that is so special about wine? What is it that makes wine potentially more protective against coronary heart disease, and possibly other diseases, than other forms of alcohol? For an answer to these questions I went to Leamington Spa in the British Midlands where, on a crisp, frosty morning, I found Professor Tom Whitehead, a rotund man in the J. B. Priestly mould, at the bottom of his garden getting ready to plant his sweet peas.

"They're a hobby of mine," he explained as he led me back to the house. Whitehead, seventy-two, is the retired dean of medicine and is emeritus professor of clinical chemistry at the University of Birmingham. But most days he's at BUPA, the insurance industry laboratories in London, where, like a handful of scientists around the world, he is using human volunteers to test the potential health benefits of wine. It was Serge Renaud's discovery of the French Paradox, Whitehead told me, that had sparked his interest in wine. (He is mainly a lager drinker himself.)

In recent years scientists have concluded that much of human disease, including cancer and the aging process itself, is caused or promoted by a group of chemicals called the "free radicals." These rogue particles prowl the body, attacking healthy cell membranes through a process called oxidation. They are the villains of our little morality play, and the knights in shining armour who attack and destroy them are called "antioxidants."

The most respected medical papers have been full of fascinating research in recent years about the role free radicals play in all sorts of diseases. But, Professor Whitehead explained, the one disease about which there is most agreement on the diabolical effect of free radicals is atherosclerosis, the hardening of the arteries.

What exactly are free radicals? Not to delve too deeply into the science of the matter, they are flawed atoms circulating in the body, each with an unpaired electron. They are highly unstable, and in their brief lifetime each makes it its business to hunt down a molecule to which it can attach that unpaired electron. When the atom finds a partner, it is whole again, but it has passed on a defect that will pass down the line in a damaging chain reaction.

Don't get me wrong. In the right place and at the right time, free radicals are lifesavers. They are natural scavenging agents, said Whitehead, that exist in our bodies and the environment. For instance, these flawed atoms help break up oil slicks in the sea after a spill, as well as the oil that wells up from the seabed in certain locations. Some free radicals also protect us by destroying bacteria in the blood. "The thing is," said Whitehead, "we've now discovered in medicine a little late in the day that we are also attacked by free radical oxygen — that we're being battered by this substance."

The oxidation process is part of our everyday life, from the rust that forms on an exposed nail to the energy we derive from breakfast when we run for the bus. It is, in short, the combining of oxygen with other chemical substances to release energy and form new compounds. Put that way, it sounds innocuous enough. But too many free radicals in our bodies, too many atoms on the loose looking for electrons with which to pair, and look out!

There are many ways in which free radicals can be released in the blood. Radiation is the classic method. Exposure to radioactive material, such as excessive X rays, releases enormous numbers of free radicals that quickly lead to radiation sickness and the other familiar terrors of the atomic age. Exposure to toxic substances also releases free radicals, which is why smoking has such an ultimately lethal effect on the system.

The body has its own defences against the ravages of free radicals in the form of three enzymes, which reduce the dangerous chemicals to harmless water. But if free radicals are produced in such numbers that they swamp the body's defences, the enzymes can't combat them; the only answer is antioxidants.

What are they? Antioxidants come in all sorts of forms, the most common of which are pills: vitamin C, vitamin E, and beta-carotene (the agent that gives carrots their orange hue). These are, of course, all readily available in our diet, especially if we eat plenty of fresh fruits and vegetables. There are also hundreds of other antioxidants used for industrial purposes as well as in foods like margarine to prevent oxidation and spoilage.

We know now that vitamin C, the virtues of which were first discovered when it was used (in the form of oranges and lemons) to cure scurvy amongst seamen, is a powerful antioxidant. And that could be why Linus Pauling, the Nobel prize — winning chemist, may have been onto something when, in 1970, he published a book advocating regular and heavy doses of vitamin C to combat the common cold. An inflammation — like a cold — will trigger the production of free radicals for protective reasons. But when the tap is not shut off, the body over-produces the scavenging cells to our overall detriment. Step in vitamin C to vanquish the little devils! (It may, incidentally, be more than chance that Pauling had reached the respectable age of ninety-three when he died in August 1994.)

Free radicals are thought to accelerate the invidious

processes of aging by attacking cell membranes and mutating the DNA — our body's blueprint — in the later years. Antioxidants, some scientists theorize, actually slow the aging process by mopping up and destroying free radicals. Whether or not antioxidants save us later on, we can be sure of one thing: we'll never get old if we die young. Sounds silly, but part of longevity is getting over the hurdle of premature death in the middle years. On that count, many reports speak favourably of antioxidants' potential for preventing cancer and other mid-life plagues. But nowhere is the impact of free radicals more telling — and the potential for using antioxidants to save and extend life more significant — than in coronary artery disease.

Remember how the "bad" cholesterol, the LDL, penetrated the artery walls to create foam cells, fatty streaks, and ultimately, plaque? On their own the LDL particles are fairly benign. It's only after being attacked by free radicals that they turn into dangerous and aggressive cells capable of penetrating and injuring the smooth walls of the arteries. Oxidized LDL is also taken up by the cells at twenty times the rate of normal LDL, substantially increasing its potential for harm. Free radicals don't just prepare the way for a heart attack; they actually make the attack much worse! During a heart attack, the heart struggles to shut off damaged and dying tissue and find alternative routes for the blood supply. According to Dr. Robert Youngson, author of *The Antioxidant Health Plan* (Thorsons, 1994), as this happens, a rush of free radicals goes on the attack. Nine or twelve hours later there is another major release of free radicals, suggesting that a lot of the worst damage in terms of weakening the heart muscle is actually done during the recovery phase.

The British Ministry of Agriculture, Fisheries and Food was so struck by the impact of free radicals in causing early deaths, particularly among men, that in 1991 it set up a $3 million research program that is even now looking at the effects of antioxidants such as vitamins C and E and beta-carotene. Most antioxidant research in the past, in fact, was concentrated on these vitamins.

"Only belatedly," said Whitehead, "have we discovered there's a group of substances called the flavonoids. They are suddenly of dramatic interest. They are ubiquitous in our foodstuffs and were first described in the 1930s." Red wine contains many phenolic substances (aromatic alcohol compounds), of which some are flavonoids — the chemicals that give the wine its special flavour and character — and many of them act as antioxidants. "Red wine," said Whitehead, "is unique in its diversity of flavonoids." Research is now directed at discovering which of the flavonoids are antioxidants.

As far as Whitehead is concerned, three studies have put the flavonoids front and centre. The first was Renaud's work on the French Paradox that suggested that wine might play an important part in overcoming the high fat diet of southwest France and protecting people there from coronary heart disease.

The second was a study by Edwin Frankel and a team at the University of California, Davis, which first demonstrated in 1993 that the flavonoids in red wine could inhibit oxidation of LDL in the blood. In that test, the scientists extracted the flavonoids from a California red wine made from Petite Sirah grapes, mixed them with blood samples from two individuals, and added copper to speed the free radical reaction. In one case, the flavonoids reduced oxidation of the LDLs by 60 percent; in the other, by a remarkable 98 percent. It meant the wine flavonoids were ten to twenty times more effective than vitamin E. The authors suggested that regular consumption of red wine showed promise of significantly reducing the incidence of coronary heart disease. Their test, they believed, also provided a plausible explanation for the French Paradox.

A third study of elderly people, undertaken in the Netherlands, identified tea, onions, and apples as major sources of flavonoids. Elderly men who consumed large amounts of these foods were found to have significantly reduced risk of coronary heart disease (CHD).

Whitehead could have added a fourth study to the list, one that provides a dramatic clue to explain the differences we noted earlier in CHD rates in different countries. Using World Health Organization figures, Professor J. Fred Gey of the University of Berne in Switzerland focused on middle-aged men in areas with high, medium, and low incidence of coronary heart disease. Among the high CHD areas were North Karelia (Finland) and Aberdeen and Edinburgh. The middle range included Belfast and Tel Aviv. The low count areas were Toulouse, Catalonia, Thun (Switzerland), and Sapri (southern Italy). Gey compared the heart attack rates with antioxidant levels in blood samples taken from men aged forty to forty-nine living in the selected areas. The result: high antioxidant levels, especially vitamin E, coincided uncannily with low heart attack rates. Vitamin E levels, in fact, were 94 percent accurate in predicting local CHD rates — a more accurate barometer than either cholesterol counts or average blood pressure figures.

It could, of course, be due to diet — as we have seen, the people of southern Europe eat more fresh fruit and vegetables than those in northern climes. But again the low heart disease profile coincided tidily with the wine-drinking areas. Coincidence? Hardly likely.

For his own study, in tracing the chain of cause and effect, Whitehead — and researchers elsewhere in the world — needed to know if the flavonoids from wine are actually absorbed into the bloodstream of living, breathing human specimens. He and his team recruited nine BUPA lab and clerical staff members, four males and five females, and told them to stay away from wine for a week in preparation for the test. At various times they were given ascorbic acid (vitamin C) with water, red wine, and white wine (both Château de Juge Bordeaux). When, on different occasions, subjects took vitamin C or drank red wine, they showed a significant rise in their antioxidant count in the following two hours; after drinking white wine, the increase in antioxidants was negligible.

The rise in antioxidant levels caused by the red wine, Whitehead concluded, "suggests that the ingestion of red wine may be a contributory factor to the French Paradox." If the effect only lasted a couple of hours, that didn't seem long enough to provide much protection. Would a glass of wine not provide twenty-four hours of protection? "I would postulate yes," replied Whitehead, "If it's red wine with a high flavonoid content." (We'll see which red wines have the most flavonoids in Chapter V.) Initially the antioxidants would saturate the areas under study, and then surplus antioxidants would be excreted. But it was his belief that protection would last at least twenty-four hours.

The difference that showed up between the red and white wine results is easily explained. "It's the skin of the grape that contains the flavonoids," said Whitehead. In the making of red wine, the skins remain in the juice, and the alcohol leaches out the flavonoids, giving the wine its characteristic flavour. With white wine, the skins are removed at the start of the process.

In studies that paralleled Whitehead's, Dr. Simon Maxwell, a lecturer in the Department of Medicine at Birmingham's Queen Elizabeth Hospital, and his colleagues gave ten students (five male, five female) red Bordeaux one day, water the next with a light lunch. Antioxidant activity levels were still elevated even four hours after ingesting the wine.

Maxwell had been struck, he told me, by the fact that people in Glasgow drink about the same amount of alcohol as people in Toulouse. "There's no question in my mind that alcohol in moderation is protective [against coronary heart disease]," he said. So that should have meant that people in the two cities would be at equal risk for coronary heart disease. Instead, as we have seen, Glasgow is amongst the worst cities in Europe for coronary heart disease, and Toulouse is one of the best. Apart from diet, said Maxwell, the difference seemed to be that beer and spirits were the drinks of choice in Glasgow, while red wine was the almost universal beverage in Toulouse.

But if antioxidant vitamins are readily available in fresh fruits and vegetables, why bother with wine? "When we got around to measuring," said Maxwell, "we found red wine has just about the most antioxidants of any fluid we have come across. It's full of flavonoids. As far as antioxidants are concerned, red wine beats the lot. It beats the others by miles."

In California, Bruce German, a colleague of Edwin Frankel's, gave me a further reason why flavonoids in wine seem to work best. Antioxidants, he said, are unstable. But in wine form, he said, the flavonoids are preserved. "They are not only concentrated, they remain intact."

Even if you buy fresh fruit and vegetables, it is no guarantee you will receive all the antioxidants you need. Vitamins are lost in travel and in storage, and vitamin C can even be depleted when you use a metal knife to cut or peel a fruit. And although studies confirm that people who consume plenty of fresh fruits and vegetables have low CHD rates, surprisingly little research has been done to establish — as is now being done with wine — how well the body can absorb and use the flavonoids in these natural products. It has been estimated that two glasses of red wine a day will enhance the flavonoid content of the average diet by 40 percent.

Most epidemiologists, though, are not yet satisfied with the evidence that wine provides better protection from coronary heart disease than beer or spirits. "And that amazes me," said Tom Whitehead. "I don't share that view at all." (I interviewed him six months before the release of the Danish epidemiological study that identified red wine as being more protective than other alcoholic beverages.) Epidemiologists, he pointed out, look at whole populations, and their emphasis is on causes of death. "It's because they haven't got the [detailed] data that they put it all down to alcohol. If alcohol was the whole answer, then the Scottish would have the lowest levels of heart disease. The French Paradox isn't only alcohol. There's more to it." In his research, he said, "we're looking at biochemical changes, so our point of view is somewhat different."

Scientists like Whitehead and Maxwell are not operating on the outer fringes of medical knowledge. In Britain they are mainstream now. A recent report by the Department of Health's Cardiovascular Review Group titled, "Nutritional Aspects of Cardiovascular Disease," had this to say:

> There is a strong inverse association between national average wine consumption and national CHD mortality . . . Alcohol consumption appears consistently to be associated with relatively low risk of CHD across a variety of studies in diverse populations . . .
>
> Some alcohol beverages contain bioactive components other than alcohol. In particular, red wine contains polyphenols which are antioxidants and capable of inhibiting LDL oxidation in vitro [in

the test tube]. Consumption of alcoholic drinks containing these compounds may contribute to the lower CHD risk in light drinkers.

The British Heart Foundation has also come onside. "A glass of red wine," said spokesperson Dr. Ian Baird in 1994, "dramatically increases the level of antioxidants in the blood in healthy volunteers. Antioxidants are believed to prevent the deposition of cholesterol in the arteries." Dr. Baird had a further good word to say for wine when I spoke to him in the fall of 1994: "It's socially acceptable to drink wine," he said. "Your chances of becoming addicted with vodka, gin, whisky, and other spirits are much greater. Go back to Hogarth on that one!" (In the eighteenth century, Hogarth's paintings depicting the social destruction caused by the gin shops helped to bring a national swing over to safer beer.)

And the evidence keeps coming. In late 1994 a team of researchers at the National Institute of Health and Nutrition in Tokyo reported what happened when they gave ten male volunteers, aged thirty-three to thirty-seven, small daily doses of vodka for a two-week period and glasses of wine (Château Lagrange) the following two weeks. When they took blood samples, they found the vodka did nothing at all to prevent oxidation of the LDL. Once the subjects switched to wine, the antioxidants went to work, and oxidation of the LDL was reduced drastically.

"Our results provide direct evidence that regular and long-term consumption of red wine, but not ethanol [alcohol], inhibited LDL oxidation," the researchers concluded. "It is suggested that red wine intake may reduce atherosclerosis and morbidity and mortality from coronary heart disease."

At what age, I asked Whitehead, should people be most concerned about seeking that antioxidant protection against atherosclerosis? For men, he said, thirty is the crucial age. "One of the things that isn't particularly recognized, and should be recognized much more, is that, in the male, cholesterol begins to rise from about thirty years of age to about fifty. That's when you're laying down your atherosclerosis and doing the damage." It peaks at about fifty-five, the time when you are most likely to have a heart attack, he said. "From thirty to fifty-five you pay attention to antioxidants and reasonable diet." For women the buildup begins at menopause. "It's a good idea to cover yourself at that time, perhaps even earlier." Should men at thirty and women at menopause consider drinking red wine for their health? "I would say so, yes," replied Whitehead. "Providing they don't take it to excess."

I left him to plant his sweet peas. In the space of a couple of hours, Dr. Whitehead had given me a valuable introduction to the exciting new world of antioxidants. But it was only a beginning.

Red wine contains a hundred or more flavonoids, and not all of them are antioxidants. Even those that are vary widely in their effectiveness, and there are serious scientific disagreements about which flavonoids work best in protecting the heart. The place to start is with resveratrol, the flavonoid found in red wine that has received the most scientific attention. And I knew the very man to talk to. My next stop would be Cornell University, in upstate New York.

RESVERATROL:
A WHISPER FROM THE ANCIENT EAST

As I entered the building, I was immediately struck by the pungent smell of apples in storage. It instantly transported me back to the apple room at Strawberry Hole, a one-time monastery in Sussex where I'd lived for a while as a boy. But it wasn't the smell I'd expected entering the portals of Cornell University. But then Leroy Creasy, the man I'd come to see, doesn't exactly fit the profile of a professor at one of the most prestigious universities in the United States either.

Creasy is a pomologist, meaning he studies fruit, and with his moustache and loud voice, he seems a bit of a country boy. He studied biochemistry at Cambridge, but you'd never know it. He comes from three generations of fruit growers in Pennsylvania, lives on a farm, makes wine with his own grapes, and prides himself on a dinner table where everything comes from his own land.

I'd first heard Creasy's name mentioned by Professor David Goldberg, a biochemist at the University of Toronto who is conducting pioneering research on the health potential of wine. In this field, Creasy's name is inescapable. You could call him the modern father of resveratrol — one of the most promising flavonoids yet discovered in wines. Creasy has devoted years to sunflower leaves, strawberries, and apples. But his big breakthrough came in the early 1980s after he began looking for natural disease-resistant agents in grape vines that would allow grape growers to use fewer chemicals in their vineyards.

"Luckily, at that time a group at the Shell Development Ltd. laboratories in England had identified a most interesting thing, a disease-resistant substance named resveratrol," said

Creasy. He couldn't understand how it had been missed earlier because it is readily visible under ultra-violet radiation. The British researchers had found "insignificant" amounts of the substance after grinding up whole grapes.

But Creasy discovered that resveratrol, a natural anti-fungicide, was contained only in the skin of the grape, which makes up only 3 or 4 percent of the weight of the fruit. Just by chance, he happened to be in the heart of resveratrol country. Fungal diseases are more prone to strike the crop in damp, cool areas, and the New York State wine-producing area close to Cornell (as well as the Burgundy and Bordeaux regions of France) fitted that specification to a tee. So when he went looking for resveratrol in the skins of locally grown grapes, he found it in much larger quantities than the British had.

At the same time, resveratrol's disease-resistant properties were being studied in Germany. Growers were already making new vine selections on the basis of resveratrol content in the leaves. They wanted plants that would not succumb to fungal diseases. And Leroy Creasy was worried. Some years earlier there had been a similar enthusiasm over a strain of disease-resistant potatoes. They were just about to go on the market when a Canadian laboratory discovered they were potentially toxic. It had been a close thing.

What if resveratrol was toxic? Little was known about it. Creasy decided to do a worldwide computer search of the scientific literature. It was a revelation. Resveratrol was nothing new. It had been known for centuries in China and Japan, where it was the base for a folk medicine called "kojo-kon." What was even more interesting, Creasy discovered there were modern labs in Japan, China, and Korea that, in recent decades, have been engaged in analyzing many old folk medicines to see if they have present-day applications. "In other words," said

Creasy, "instead of eating the guts of some strange snake, you could synthesize the chemical involved and give it to people in more acceptable form."

In the 1930s a laboratory had identified resveratrol as coming from *veratrum Formosa*, a lily. In the 1960s there was another Far East flurry of interest in resveratrol, with a number of animal experiments being conducted. Creasy was fascinated to discover that kojo-kon had been prescribed for athlete's foot — a fungal complaint. Even more interesting to those now exploring wine's apparent potential for reducing coronary heart disease, it had also been prescribed by the ancients for atherosclerosis and inflammatory diseases. Instead of extracting resveratrol from the skins of grapes, the folk doctors had got their supply by grinding up the roots of *polygonum cuspidatum*, known to exasperated modern-day gardeners as the unstoppable Japanese knotweed. Creasy calls it "a beast of a weed."

The modern Far East research showed those old folk doctors knew what they were about. Tests involving rodents showed that resveratrol was an antioxidant that boosted HDL cholesterol and broke down the agents that are precursors of life-threatening fatty deposits in the arteries. One lab had even taken out a patent on resveratrol, although that does not seem to have hampered current research.

The mainly Japanese research ended in the mid-1980s. The scientists had apparently not realized resveratrol was also available in one of the most widely consumed beverages in the world — wine. But Creasy had an inkling. He had tested some wines for resveratrol in the early 1980s — with meagre results. The wines used were "free run," which meant the grapes were only lightly processed rather than squeezed. Then he tried again, primarily with red wines. His idea was that wines offered the perfect "living library" for keeping track of resveratrol content. The label on the bottle usually told you where the grapes were grown and when. It was a perfect cataloguing system for keeping track of resveratrol counts from year to year and from place to place. And he started testing wines from Bordeaux and California as well as New York State for their resveratrol content.

The pace was picking up. In Bordeaux, a team headed by a researcher named Martine Segneur reported in 1991 on their results after administering alcohol, white wine, and red wine to sixteen male subjects over fifteen-day periods. They showed that red wine increased the "good" HDL cholesterol and reduced the "stickiness" of platelets. It was another clue. Some scientists have expressed reservations over a second Segneur finding that alcohol increased the harmful LDL count. Other studies contradict this finding.

In 1992, in a paper published in an obscure journal of viticulture, Creasy and a colleague, E. H. Siemann, established the resveratrol content of twenty-nine wines, most from New York or California, a few from France. By the standards of tests now going on elsewhere, their equipment and methods were primitive, and the amounts they were measuring were small. But already a general pattern was discernible.

White wines, to begin with, contained very little resveratrol. Red wines contained, typically, fifty to one hundred times as much as white wines. But the resveratrol content of red wines also varied widely, depending on the species of grape, the geographical origin of the wine, and the processing methods. Significantly, a 1988 red Bordeaux registered by far the highest resveratrol count, while a 1982 California Cabernet Sauvignon, a grape that in the right climate and conditions has a high resveratrol content, had close to a zero reading. It could have been that, since the California wine was much older, the resveratrol had broken down and disappeared, the authors speculated.

In comparisons of California Chardonnays with those from New York State, the New York wines contained "significantly more resveratrol." It was not hard to understand why. New York's moist growing climate puts its grape harvest "under higher fungal disease pressure," whereas in California's sunny, mostly dry climate, the grapes have less need for an anti-fungal agent to fight off disease.

This was more than a simple scientific finding; this was a declaration of war. In 1993 California produced over a billion litres of wine worth $7.2 billion, accounting for 90 percent of U.S. wine production. The big California growers didn't want to hear that some *apple* professor in upstate New York had discovered a wonderful new health boon in wine — and that their wine, which was mostly white, was almost devoid of it. As Creasy puts it with notable understatement, "California producers are a little less enthusiastic about resveratrol than European producers."

In France and Italy, scientists in the pomology field were already exploring the possibilities of resveratrol. But Creasy's findings might have gone generally unnoticed outside the wine business — if they hadn't been overtaken by the French Paradox tidal wave. By the date of the *60 Minutes* broadcast, word had leaked out about Creasy's resveratrol findings (they wouldn't be published for another month). He was in hot demand for interviews, and his discoveries received wide exposure in the European media.

It's not hard to see why. Up to that point nearly all the favourable findings about alcohol and wine had been based on population studies. That was a bit vague. Here at last was someone who could point to an actual substance in wine and say, on the basis of the Japanese experiments, what exactly it did to combat coronary artery disease. Soon Creasy was receiving phone calls from ordinary people all over the United States, asking him whether they should drink red wine for the sake of their hearts.

"People were calling me who had never drunk wine in their lives," he said with amazement. His invariable advice is, don't drink wine as medicine: drink it only if you enjoy it. And then drink it with meals and in moderation and you'll have nothing to worry about. And if you want to be sure to get your share of those important phenolics, drink a different red wine each night, he advises.

His encounters with the great numbers of people who don't drink wine have made him impatient with the industry squabbles. He doesn't give a hoot whether California wine producers have their noses out of joint because their wines don't contain much resveratrol. They should be more concerned, he says, about the fact that so few people in the northern countries — and especially in the United States — drink wine at all. "My sense is, if you could get 5 percent of people drinking red wine with their meal, then maybe 1 percent would start having a glass of white wine before their meal." In that way the whole wine industry would benefit, he says.

Since he and Siemann published their paper, controversy has raged over whether it is resveratrol, or some of the other one hundred and more phenolic substances in wine, that provides the most significant protection against coronary heart disease. Creasy still believes firmly in resveratrol. Why? "It's the only substance in wine that has obvious, proven medical benefits." Proven, even his critics would have to admit, over several centuries.

Quercetin: Frog Turns into Prince

Resveratrol was not the only antioxidant being studied. In the late 1970s, scientists were already looking at quercetin (kwer-sit-in), a substance found in nearly all our fruits and vegetables, as well as in red wine. But then came the bad news: quercetin had been found to be cancer-causing. It had failed the Ames Test, a widely accepted test developed by Berkeley professor Bruce Ames for identifying mutagens — cancer-causing agents.

Quercetin is present in many of our foods, especially in green onions or shallots, in red and yellow onions, leeks, and garlic. It is also found in grapes. If it caused cancer, the consequences could hardly be contemplated. Quercetin is so ubiquitous it is almost impossible to avoid. And it appears in greatest abundance in the very foods — fruits and vegetables — that we have been urged to consume for our health.

Scientists are not supposed to panic, but there was definitely a feeling of, let's say, unease. And then came the good news. Tests on animals and cell cultures showed the deadly result was caused by what scientists call, "an artifact of the laboratory testing system." Which means it was just a quirky result related to the nature of the test and had nothing to do with the way quercetin behaved when it was consumed in the human body.

Ames, busy on other projects, told a younger colleague, Terrance Leighton, "This looks interesting. Care to check into it?" Which is how Leighton, a professor of biochemistry and molecular biology, became Professor Quercetin to the world. After conducting more sophisticated tests, he was soon able to say with confidence, "Quercetin does not give any significant evidence of gene toxicity."

And then the news got better still: "What we found out was that quercetin actually acts as an anticarcinogen — an anti-cancer agent." Leighton can still laugh at this amazing, "frog into prince" turnaround.

When I spoke to him in early 1995, he explained that when breast and colon cancers were artificially induced in mice, quercetin stopped the tumours in their tracks and blocked their development. It also blocked the activity of compounds that promote cancer growth. In other words, it could turn off cancer before it got started. Just to be sure, tests have been done over and over again at the Georgetown University Cancer Center in which quercetin treatments stop the development of cancers in mice. Once the quercetin treatment is suspended, the tumours resume their growth.

It was found especially effective, said Leighton, in stopping or preventing cancer of the colon. In tests at the Sloan-Kettering Cancer Center, in New York, quercetin and rutin, another flavonoid found widely in fruits and vegetables as well as in red wine, were both able to "suppress tumour multiplicity and, ultimately, tumour development," with quercetin having a slight edge over rutin.

But can it do for humans what it undoubtedly does for mice? The only answer so far comes from a U.S. National Cancer Institute study in China that showed that people on a high-quercetin diet — including a lot of onions and garlic — experienced a 30 to 40 percent lower incidence of cancers in the alimentary canal — the digestive tract from mouth to anus. If it's so effective, government science agencies must be falling over each other to get the necessary studies done and get the word out to the public, right? Not at all.

Leighton had a by now familiar story to tell me. "The National Institute of Health [which sets the research priorities] doesn't have much interest in diet-cancer relationships, or diet and health relationships in general," he said, trying to keep the bitterness out of his voice. There are, he said, countless studies pointing to quercetin as an important substance in the prevention or containment of cancer. All that's needed now is a full clinical study. "But I don't think anybody's going to do it." Why? "Because there's no money to be made," he replied simply.

Even though it's known that diet is a major contributing factor to cancer and other diseases, the medical establishment, he said, is still obsessed by the "magic bullet" approach where one elusive drug will be found to cure all cancers. "They are looking for a pharmaceutical solution," he said.

The prize, of course, is huge. Pharmaceutical companies would make stupendous profits from such a find. But meanwhile there's little interest in the branch of knowledge now known as "nutri-ceuticals" — because you can't make money telling people to eat shallots and leeks. Leighton estimates it would cost $300 to $400 million to carry out the kind of full-scale clinical studies that might establish quercetin's potential for preventing or containing, for instance, breast cancer or skin cancer. "It may be done in Europe," he said, "But I don't think it's likely to happen in the United States or Canada."

If you believe Leighton, what it amounts to is that, in the absence of properly funded research into dietary aspects of disease, you and I, as concerned laypeople, need to find the best information available and act for our own protection — ensuring only that we are not exposing ourselves to danger.

What are the hard facts on quercetin? Undoubtedly the highest amounts are to be found in the *Allium* vegetables — the onions, garlic, and leeks we've mentioned. How much of the quercetin from these sources is absorbed into the body is not known. Laboratory and animal tests, said Leighton, show "that the levels that are found in wine are pharmacologically significant." In other words, there's enough to do you some good.

Because quercetin is hydrophobic — doesn't like being in water — it may well be, he said, that it is more readily absorbed by the body in an ethanol solution (in wine) than it is in vegetable form. Again, more research is needed. Again, there's no money for it. But after checking the quercetin content of some five hundred wines, Leighton at least now knows a good deal about where to find it and how it behaves in wine form.

Like a number of other flavonoids in wine, quercetin is an antioxidant that protects the DNA and chases down the free radicals that contribute to coronary heart disease. And like them, it is found in the skin of the grape. As a result, it is found only in red wine, where the wine is fermented with the skins, and not in white because there the skins are removed from the start.

Where resveratrol, a natural anti-fungal agent and one of the significant flavonoids found in wine, flourishes in cool, damp climates like that found in France, Ontario, or Oregon, and New York State, quercetin is a sun-lover. Quercetin, said Leighton, is formed by ultraviolet light. "The more direct or filtered sunshine gets on the fruit, the more quercetin you get. With a really shaded crop, you find less of it."

Unlike resveratrol, which is found in greatest concentration in certain grape species, quercetin is not specific to species. The amount of sunshine, said Leighton, seems to be the only factor in determining quercetin levels in the grape. Beyond that, the eventual quercetin content of the wine, he said, depends almost exclusively on the techniques used in making the wine. The length of time the wine is left in contact with the skins, first of all, determines how much is extracted.

But here's a fascinating finding: even a high quercetin reading may not signify much because the substance at that point is not in a form in which it can be absorbed. It is inactive. Only when it is allowed to remain for a time with the yeast leftovers — a common practice in traditional wineries — does it convert to active quercetin. If that doesn't happen, fear not! All is not lost.

"What we have shown," said Leighton, "is that there are bacteria in your gut that carry out the same reaction — converting the inactive quercetin to the active form. But this reaction only occurs in the lower portion of the alimentary tract." It's an interesting proposition: Are you better off with active quercetin from fully processed wine, which may benefit the stomach and the upper reaches of the digestive system, and which may also be absorbed to attack the free radicals rampaging through the arterial system? Or is it a better bet to go with inactive quercetin, which glides unchallenged through the system, until it reaches the large intestine where it can be converted and go right to work doing one of the jobs it's best fitted for: preventing colon cancer?

These are the sorts of delicious questions scientists relish, and so far there is no clear answer. Quercetin faces another hazard in the wine-making process. Many large, "cost-conscious" wineries, said Leighton, press their grapes to extract every last possible drop of juice. The result is a wine containing so many tannins and phenolic substances that it is bitter to the taste. To make it palatable, the large wineries use a product called PVPP, a fining agent (it removes solid matter) that gets rid of the bitterness — as well as the phenolics, including quercetin. In fact, the end product, designed to sell cheaply, to look like wine, and maybe even to smell and taste a little bit like wine, has none of the health benefits we've talked about in this book. Other fining agents and even micro-filters, said Leighton, do not seem to have much effect on quercetin content, although these techniques can remove resveratrol and other flavonoids.

Unlike resveratrol, which seems to disappear the older a wine gets, quercetin is long-lived. "We have looked at wines twenty and thirty years old, and it seems to be very stable," said Leighton. Good news for cooks too: it is unaffected by normal cooking temperatures.

Leighton is naturally frustrated at the lack of official attention being paid to "nutri-ceuticals." It's particularly ironic, he says, when there is so much talk of trying to reduce medical costs. Changing people's diet, he said, "is one of the leverage points. It would not be hard to do."

But it's not all bad news. You don't need a prescription from the doctor to change your diet. Or the approval of a pharmaceutical company. "It's under the control of every individual," said Leighton. "And it could have substantial effects on chronic disease outcomes." In that light, flavonoids, and quercetin in particular, "are extremely interesting."

THE WORD FROM CALIFORNIA: WINE AS A FOOD

The studies looking at the health-protective benefits of flavonoids have brought about a new way of thinking. As Selwyn St. Leger, the British scientist who first connected wine and cardiovascular health, had said to me in Manchester, "we should think of wine as a food. A special sort of food." That is exactly the new thinking about wine that the university town of Davis, California, promotes.

In early 1995, I made my way there through torrential northern California rain. I passed vineyards and ditches under water, dry riverbeds that had turned into raging torrents, and finally parked on Davis's main street and fled through the rain into Kings restaurant. "Nonsmoking section, please," I said. The host smiled at me archly. "No one smokes in Davis, sir," he said. And I remembered that this city south of Sacramento is famous these days for two things. One, probably the severest antismoking law in the world, prohibiting smoking in the bars, and even on the sidewalk within twenty feet of any public building. And two, the University of California, Davis, whose Department of Viticulture and Enology, one of the world's leading wine research centres.

The healthful attributes of wine are nothing new to Davis. In fact, when I paid a courtesy visit on Vern Singleton, a seventy-one-year-old retired viticulture professor, he was a little bitter about it. Singleton wrote a textbook in 1969 explaining wine phenolics. "It bothers me," he said, as we sipped a dry California sherry while contemplating the downpour outside, "that I spent thirty-three years in this line, and nobody paid a bit of attention to me."

Vern didn't even follow his own advice about wine's benefits. "It was a rare meal where we had wine," he admitted. "I didn't drink it regularly even though I was teaching that it was good for you." It may just be coincidence, but Vern is now a victim of atherosclerosis. He was recovering from a heart bypass operation when I spoke to him.

By next morning the rain had stopped, and the university campus was fragrant with the smell of blossoms. Vern Singleton's successors suffer from no lack of attention these days. The names of scientists like Andrew Waterhouse and Edwin Frankel are familiar wherever the issue of wine and health is debated. But Bruce German, a Canadian who is an associate professor of food sciences at Davis, best explained the philosophy that, the people at Davis hope, will change the minds of governments and the public on the issue of drinking for health.

Government food policies around the world, he said, have all in the past been directed towards getting people to the age of reproduction — their teens or early twenties. After that, in nutritional terms, governments lose interest. Think about it for a minute: there is a huge historical emphasis on milk and other dairy products as nutrients — when it's realized now that they mainly benefit children (and perhaps not even them) and are directly linked with high coronary rates later in life. For decades all the emphasis has been on bouncier babies, bigger adolescents — and the end result has turned out to be a North American epidemic of adult obesity leading to ill health, unhappiness, and, frequently, early death from stroke, heart disease, or cancer. According to German, provided that you live to twenty, governments in the past were simply not interested in getting you to eighty.

That's changing. The British government's 1994 Committee on the Medical Aspects of Food Policy (COMA) report made a powerful plea to the public to cut back on fats, and eat more bread, fruits, and vegetables. But that's still rather conventional "eat your veggies" stuff. There hasn't, said German, been much interest shown in anything that could be considered "nonessential" nutrients — like wine. "What I care about is being at an optimal nutritional status for the next forty years," he stated. And for that to happen generally, more attention must be paid to the chemicals that sustain our health throughout life. With a rapidly aging population, German sees it as an issue that will only grow in importance.

So what are the chemicals that could improve our lives? Antioxidants, said German, are a prime example. And that, of course, is why wine, in the view of German and Waterhouse and others at Davis, should be looked at from a nutritional point of view.

In the early stages of my research, especially after talking to Professor Leroy Creasy, "the father of resveratrol," I had regarded the search for the protective agent in wine as a sort of horse race. Resveratrol took a lead in the early running, but in the back stretch other antioxidants with names like quercetin and catechin were coming up fast. In the final bend resveratrol was still making a good run, but as they approach the post . . . In the intervening months, though, events had been moving quickly. Now, rather than a horse race with a single, clear winner, it was looking more and more as if the antioxidants in wine work like a team of Clydesdales, all working in harmony.

"The key," said Andrew Waterhouse, assistant professor of enology at Davis, "is that each chemical is an antioxidant in a certain situation." Vitamin E, for example, is fat soluble, and finds its way into the LDL cholesterol, whereas vitamin C is water soluble, and is never found in the fat. To make it more complicated, the two vitamins seem to work together to prevent oxidation. In wine making, sulphur dioxide and ascorbic acid (vitamin C) each cause browning when they are added to the crushed grapes. But if they are added together, they prevent the crushed fruit and juice from browning.

When Waterhouse's people analyze red wine, they commonly find fifty or more flavonoids, and they are only beginning to understand how they work singly and together on the human system. "We're looking at the activity of as many substances as we can get our hands on," said Waterhouse. See what I mean about a team of horses.

Edwin Frankel and Bruce German established in 1993 that resveratrol can, in a test tube, inhibit the oxidation of human LDL — a vital step in preventing coronary artery disease. But, they pointed out, resveratrol was only present in small amounts (a problem aggravated by the fact that they used California wine, which rarely contains much resveratrol). The Davis people have also confirmed that the anti-cancer agent, quercetin, as well as epicatechin, another flavonoid found in wine that may also have cancer-fighting capability, are active antioxidants.

In one paper, Waterhouse and Frankel pointed out that, although the U.S. government recommends healthy servings of legumes, grains, vegetables, and fruit, it's difficult to change people's eating habits. Americans, for example, have been told to eat five servings of fruits and vegetables a day — a forlorn hope in light of the fact that, like people everywhere in the developed world, Americans are opting for processed and fast foods. Two glasses of wine, though, would boost the average U.S. dietary level of antioxidants by 40 percent, according to the Davis researchers.

It is quite possible, said Waterhouse, that as the beneficial effects of some of the antioxidants are accepted, it will be practical to tailor wines to boost their healthful properties. But there is still a great deal of research to be done on wine and, due to the deep government suspicion about any findings that might be favourable towards alcohol, they face a chronic shortage of research funds.

Like David Goldberg in Toronto and Tom Whitehead and Simon Maxwell in England, the Davis team is eager to show that wine antioxidants can actually be absorbed into the human system. The day I was there, they were, in a professionally correct manner, cock-a-hoop at the results of a test on catechin, the most abundant of the antioxidants in wine that has been shown to inhibit the "clumping" or aggregation of platelets.

Four individuals, including German, were put on the gruesome North American high-fat, fast-food diet to purge their systems of any beneficial antioxidants they might have derived from fresh fruits and vegetables. Then they were given small quantities of catechin-high wine (in tests on twenty California wines for catechin, a Petite Sirah was a top scorer, followed by a Zinfandel). Catechin levels in their blood zoomed up quite satisfactorily. Half had disappeared after eighteen hours. Once again, reported the team, the French Paradox had been substantiated — it was the regular, modest consumption of wine that made the difference. If you do all your wine drinking on Saturday night, instead of spreading it out over the week, said German, it probably means you are without the antioxidant protection 80 percent of the time.

How certain is it then that red wine prevents coronary heart disease? I got two answers. The alcohol in the wine, said German, clearly provides protection. Beyond that, "the phenolics make the big difference. In the research we have done, they are not only effective as antioxidants, but they work to inhibit the production of enzymes that promote clotting and the aggregation of platelets. So there are multiple targets for these phenolics." Their protective qualities have been demonstrated in the test tube, he said, and it would be hard to believe that, if they were present in the body in sufficient quantities, the same beneficial effects would not be the result.

Waterhouse was more cautious. Epidemiological evidence that wine protects against coronary heart disease (St. Leger and other studies) is strong, he said. But so far the antioxidant effect of the flavonoids has only been proven in test tubes, using human plasma. At present, while it's possible to demonstrate the presence of the antioxidants in the blood following intakes of wine, there is no way to show in vivo — in living, breathing subjects — that the antioxidants are chasing down and destroying free radicals. The wine and health issue is, in some ways, where the cigarette and health issue has been for nearly fifty years. In the case of tobacco, epidemiological and animal studies showed over and over again the harmful effects of smoking. But it would have been unethical to carry out a human study in which half the subjects were directed to smoke and half were not.

Waterhouse is confident that, once they have an absolutely clear picture of how wine phenolics work in the human system, it will be possible to mount a large-scale study, involving thousands of people. But it will be expensive, he warns, and may take years. But he couldn't resist a small, wistful hope: "If we can reduce heart disease by 10 or 20 percent, well, that's a huge benefit."

JOHN IREX'S AWKWARD QUESTION

It started with a phone call from a customer. John Irex called with a question that Alex Karumanchiri, head of the laboratories at the Liquor Control Board of Ontario (LCBO), could not answer. Irex, a retired importer of surgical instruments and wine enthusiast, had heard about the French Paradox and had a very simple question: "If wine is good for you, which wines are best?"

Karumanchiri was stumped. It was no wonder he didn't have an answer. At that time — 1993 — hardly any research had been done on the subject. Leroy Creasy had tested a number of wines, most of them from New York State, but his equipment was primitive and the amounts of the flavonoid resveratrol he had found in the wines was disappointing.

Despite the lack of information, neither Irex nor

Karumanchiri wanted to drop the subject. They had more talks, finally met, and became friends. One day Irex said, "There's someone I think you should meet." The irrepressible Irex, who calls himself an "amateur du vin," had got chatting in Vintages, the Ontario government's vintage wine shop, to another wine enthusiast, University of Toronto professor of biochemistry David Goldberg.

Professor Goldberg, chairman of the Canadian Atherosclerosis Society education committee, had first started examining alcohol's potential for preventing coronary heart disease fifteen years earlier. He was as interested in Irex's question as Karumanchiri had been. It wasn't long before Karumanchiri introduced a friend of his, George Soleas, chairman of the technical committee of the Canadian Wine Institute, to Goldberg. And the work began.

They were an unlikely trio to be uncorking new secrets from the drink of the ancients. There wasn't an aristocratic French name amongst them, and their work would be done not on the sun-baked shores of the Mediterranean, where wine is a way of life, but on the chilly northern shores of Lake Ontario. Goldberg, born in Glasgow, got his taste for fine wine when he was president of the Student Union at the University of Glasgow: he discovered his duties included attending wine tastings to make selections for Union dinners. He was not remiss in his duties.

Soleas, of Greek-Cypriot background, grew up with wine; he was working for a steel company when he learned that Andrés, one of Canada's biggest wine companies, was looking for a biochemist. He prepared himself by studying with the wine experts at the University of California at Davis. Now, working from his lab set amongst vineyards half an hour up the road from Niagara Falls, he is consumed by wine's possibilities.

Karumanchiri, a novel writer and tennis player in his spare time, is a superb cook who, as a boy growing up in Southern India, learned the art from the family chef, a man who had been in charge of galleys on the great liners.

Goldberg was intrigued by the possibilities of resveratrol. As did Leroy Creasy, Goldberg had discovered that the Japanese were studying resveratrol for treatment of atherosclerosis. And he was interested in resveratrol for another reason. Many flavonoids, such as quercetin, are found commonly in fruits and vegetables and other items in our diet. But resveratrol is found in wine and in almost nothing else that we eat or drink (except peanuts). It was tempting to believe that it was one of the key ingredients in providing the French with their special cloak of protection.

For one of their first moves, Goldberg and Soleas drove to upstate New York for a memorable meal on Creasy's farm. His wife, Minn, had shot the venison she served. Creasy, as they discussed resveratrol's possibilities, served wine he'd made with his own grapes (which, coming from that region, would certainly have had a high resveratrol count). Back in Toronto, at his office in the Banting Institute, a gaunt old place named for Fred Banting, the co-discoverer of insulin, Goldberg devised a series of experiments to put resveratrol to the test, in some cases on human subjects.

He intended to test the effects of resveratrol on blood coagulation in the test tube, comparing it with quercetin and other phenolics. In addition, he recruited twenty-four young, male volunteers who would, in succession and over a period of weeks, consume ordinary commercial grape juice; juice fortified with resveratrol; white wine; and a red wine with a high resveratrol content.

Soleas and Karumanchiri, meanwhile, addressed themselves

to John Irex's question. They wanted to know which wines had the highest resveratrol content. Old test methods were painfully slow. Weeks of work might produce test results on a dozen or so wines. They examined and discarded several test methods, then hit on a system of chromatography analysis — the kind of thing you see on TV police procedural shows when they're talking about drug or blood analysis — that opened the flood gates. Suddenly they were able to test whole batches of wine for resveratrol.

The tests were quick and the results, measured against other procedures, proved accurate. Karumanchiri had a major advantage over university researchers in the field: he had unlimited access to wines from all over the world for test purposes. The LCBO, as the largest wine purchaser in the world, is constantly testing the wines it buys. In a surprisingly short time the team had data on two hundred, then three hundred, and soon more than nine hundred wines. And the resveratrol story was there plain to see.

As expected, resveratrol showed up almost exclusively in red wines. The often cloudy skies of the Burgundy and Bordeaux regions of France, as well as the mist-shrouded vineyards of Switzerland and Oregon, proved particularly hospitable to damp-loving resveratrol. Wines from hotter, sunnier climes like those in Italy, Spain, Australia, and California didn't fare as well.

There was a little bit of hope for everyone, though. Grape varieties turned out to be just as important as the region of origin when it came to resveratrol counts. Wine made from Pinot Noir, the single dull, dark grape that originated in Burgundy and that makes some of the finest wine in the world, registered high resveratrol counts regardless of where the grapes were grown. It is not the easiest grape to cultivate, but today growers in Germany, Eastern Europe, California, Oregon, Australia, New Zealand, and Canada are all learning its finicky ways. Merlot, Gamay, and Shiraz were also grape varieties that seemed to do well wherever they were grown.

Cabernet Sauvignon, however, was less able to surmount the climatic barriers. The beloved little "Cab," tough as shoe leather and redolent with tannins and aroma, was superb, in resveratrol terms, in the Bordeaux region, but less successful in Australia and many other New World wine-producing areas.

The varietal results gave some encouragement to growers outside France. The French have long held the world in awe of its wines as the best, the ultimate. It would be too much to swallow if, with the emphasis switching to the health aspects of wine, the French were once again able to claim a monopoly — a resveratrol monopoly.

If resveratrol indeed proves to be one of the most important flavonoids in wine, then products from Burgundy and Bordeaux will rank high on the health scale. But by concentrating on the right grape varieties (principally Pinot Noir), producers in hotter climates — Spain, Italy, California, and many of the other New World wine-producing countries — can avoid being locked out. The very highest counts recorded in the LCBO tests, in fact, were for Pinot Noirs from Switzerland, Oregon, and Ontario.

But there was still a big doubt regarding resveratrol. When I spoke to Andrew Waterhouse in California in the autumn of 1994, he said, "It's my feeling now that resveratrol is a minor component in the big picture. The problem is there's so little of it in wine. Other phenolic substances are much more abundant." But even as we talked, things were happening. At the LCBO labs it was noted that when a fresh assay of resveratrol was prepared, a single peak appeared. As the assay aged, a second peak would appear. The original is called trans-resveratrol, the new peak, cis-resveratrol. It meant there was more resveratrol than had been suspected. Since then two glucosides of resveratrol (glucose molecules attached to resveratrol) have been discovered, and Karumanchiri believes there may be other forms yet to be found. Tests today are showing levels of resveratrol forty or fifty times as high as those recorded by Creasy — enough, Goldberg believes, to be clinically significant.

Happily, the good news about resveratrol has been confirmed by an Italian scientist, Dr. Fulvio Mattivi, who has been experimenting with the substance for several years. His latest tests also show that some wines from Italy and other warmer climes contain the useful glucosides of resveratrol. When I spoke to him late in 1994, Dr. Mattivi was about to commence full-scale tests on volunteers, testing one phenolic product at a time, and measuring antioxidant activity.

In his laboratory at the University of Toronto, meanwhile, Goldberg's tests on volunteers were showing once again that resveratrol boosted HDL at the expense of the potentially damaging LDL cholesterol. His subjects, aged twenty-one to forty-five, first abstained from alcohol of any sort for two weeks, then consumed regular commercial grape juice for four weeks, followed by resveratrol-fortified juice for four weeks. Two weeks of abstinence followed, to clear the resveratrol from the system, and to prepare for the final four weeks drinking one glass of white wine a day and four weeks drinking one glass of a red wine high in resveratrol a day.

While the red wine produced the highest levels of "good" HDL, plain grape juice, because of its high sugar content, actually had an adverse effect, lowering HDL levels. When resveratrol was added to the juice, the adverse effect was reversed, essentially bringing the subjects back to the point from which they started. Clearly resveratrol has its maximum effect in wine. The fermentation process frees the resveratrol, making it available to our bodies when we sip a glass of red wine.

One difficulty in testing, said Goldberg, is that there is an overlap in the resveratrol benefit and the overall benefit that comes from alcohol. He will attempt to isolate the respective benefits to a greater degree in future tests. His mission: to check on the effectiveness not only of trans-resveratrol, but also of several other antioxidants and wine phenolics on platelet aggregation. It all sounds rather obscure, but translated into everyday terms, it means he is looking for the agent most likely to keep the blood flowing and prevent the clots that cause heart attacks or strokes.

Vitamin E and the other antioxidants did nothing to slow down the tendency for the platelets to clump together. Neither did two wine phenolics, catechin and its sister, epicatechin. The star performers were our old friend, the cancer-stopper quercetin, and trans-resveratrol.

The two flavonoids each inhibited coagulation in several different ways and generally more effectively than pure alcohol. What was especially intriguing was that they did so through different chemical pathways. Trans-resveratrol, says Goldberg, is the only agent that blocks the production of thromboxin, which is the most powerful of the chemicals promoting platelet aggregation. It appears that quercetin attacks the symptoms, while resveratrol attacks the cause. "In preventing coagulation," he said, following the in vitro tests, "resveratrol is the most powerful of the flavonoids we have tested."

In the complex chemical process of atherosclerosis, the white blood cells also play a wrecking role. When there is a bacterial infection, these cells secrete chemicals that cause an inflammatory reaction in the arteries. They are, in effect, local hormones, signalling to attract other white cells to the inflamed area. The end results are obstruction and a potential clot.

Once again, trans-resveratrol, says Goldberg, blocks production of the potentially harmful secretions in vitro more effectively than any of the other phenolics yet tested. Goldberg's results for his male volunteers, however, were not as clear-cut. White wine performed as well or even a little better in suppressing some of the processes that lead to platelet aggregation and clots. He believes now the results may have been compromised by the difficulties with the testing procedure. Final word awaits the results of experiments now being conducted by Mattivi and others.

Was it a good idea anyway to bet just on resveratrol? However promising the results, several other flavonoids, including quercetin, catechin, and epicatechin, each make their special contribution to healthy arteries. In California, Andrew Waterhouse and his team were showing catechin, which is actually the most abundant of the flavonoids, could be absorbed into the bloodstream. If resveratrol was a marker for all the other flavonoids, in other words, if a high resveratrol count automatically meant the other flavonoids were present in quantity, then all you needed to measure was resveratrol. But as we have already seen with quercetin, that wasn't always the case. With California wines in particular — naturally low in resveratrol because of the warm, dry climate — quercetin was often present where resveratrol was absent in a sort of seesaw effect. And although the Toronto trio was finding resveratrol in amounts far greater than had earlier been the case, the amounts were still small compared with catechin.

Resveratrol needed to pack a significant punch if it really was the wonder ingredient. It was time for the trio to hedge its bets. Goldberg prepared to carry out lab tests using catechin, while Karumanchiri and Soleas looked at expanding their wine-testing procedures to take in the other flavonoids. Again technical wizardry won the day. After going through three different versions, they came up with a liquid chromatography method that allowed them to test extracts of wine at room temperature (instead of heating the wine extracts as they'd had to do with their resveratrol tests), producing measurements for a range of flavonoids at double-quick speed.

Again, they'd taken a dramatic lead in the field. What they found may, as the health benefits of wine become recognized, have important implications for wine-making around the world. Whatever the country, it was usually small wineries using traditional techniques that produced wine with the highest flavonoid content. "Generally, the best wine in the world is produced in small wineries," said Karumanchiri. "They can pay more attention to details and to traditions. They have the knowledge of centuries of wine-making. Each one has learned a little trick of getting a special flavour and they will not compromise."

The large wineries were often another story. And they weren't entirely to blame if the phenolics in their wine went missing — that's exactly the way many customers want their wine. Unsophisticated wine purchasers want a product that's crystal clear. To achieve that, many wineries now use a process called "chill filtering." It is what the name suggests: the temperature of the wine is brought down, making it easier to filter out any particulate matter as well as "wine diamonds" — the perfectly harmless crystals formed by sugar. Unfortunately, filtering often removes the flavonoids that do us good. Even normal filtering, said George Soleas as he took me on a tour of the Andrés Winery, removes 50 percent of the phenolics, and charcoal filtering, used to clarify the colour of some wines, removes 70 or 80 percent of the resveratrol in a wine.

For example, Pinot Noir, the grape that scores high on the resveratrol table wherever it's grown, isn't immune to the inroads of the filters. "Just recently," said Karumanchiri, "we tested a Pinot Noir from a major winery that is notorious for filtering." It had almost no resveratrol. "If it had come from any other winery, I would have said perhaps there had been a mistake," he said.

White wines in particular must be clear as well water before most customers will accept them. Sediment in the bottom would be considered a scandal. As a result, said Soleas, white wine is not fermented "on the skins." The skins, and all the phenolics they contain, are generally used for fertilizer. It wouldn't be difficult, he believes, to extract the phenolics from the skins and add them to the white wine — a development that would put white wines on a par with the reds in health terms. Some people in the industry are also considering adding vitamin C — a potent antioxidant — to their wines.

It's easier to accept red wines with sediment (containing the phenolics that nature intended). Indeed, at the Robert Mondavi winery in the Napa Valley I saw bottles that are now plainly labelled "Unfiltered." But, said Soleas, it's a matter of price — and sophistication. "If people pay $7 for a bottle of wine and find sediment, they complain. If they pay $27, they don't complain."

It's hardly likely that the big wineries will abandon the homogenized brand-name products they produce for the mass market. Instead, as consumers become aware of the health benefits — and the flavour — they're losing, Karumanchiri believes the big wineries will start producing more and more unfiltered "boutique" wines aimed directly at the health-conscious.

But what is the answer to John Irex's question? We won't get a full picture of how the antioxidants in wine work singly and together to protect us from heart disease for several years yet. But Chapter V gives guidelines and general examples for choosing wines that can help protect you from heart trouble.

THE GREAT WINE FLAVONOID STAKES

As we've seen, antioxidants may work as a team offering different sorts of protection. But it might be fun to call it a horse race after all — the Great Flavonoid Stakes. And this is how the most promising runners line up at the starting gate today.

Resveratrol: game little filly, antecedents go back centuries. Small in stature but a real runner. Outstanding in coagulation for the two reasons we have seen, a proven inhibitor of LDL cholesterol and booster of the good stuff, HDL.

Quercetin: call her "Wrong-Way Rose," a difficult horse that started out running in the wrong direction. Now she's on track and a double threat — both in combatting atherosclerosis and knocking off villainous cancer. Like resveratrol, she counters platelet aggregation and is also a powerful antioxidant. Good all-rounder.

Catechin: big, rangy stallion, sheer size carries him through. Present in greater abundance than other helpful phenolics, good antioxidant action, but falls down when it comes to stopping platelet aggregation. Main strong point: as an antioxidant. The same goes for epicatechin.

Dark horses: Rutin, a glucoside of quercetin, gallic acid, cyanidin, and myricetin. They're off!

CHAPTER V

Finding the Wines That Help Most

WHICH WINES TO PICK

Shopping for a bottle of wine in any sort of large wine or liquor store these days is a daunting experience. The wine market exploded in the prosperous eighties, and today the dazzled consumer is faced with an overwhelming choice of wines. Many are old favourites; many others are new-comers from countries you never even dreamed had a wine industry. What makes picking a wine even more difficult is that a lot of the new products are actually very good. New World wineries (meaning outside Europe) in such regions as Australia, Chile, and definitely California are producing wines that compare favourably — or even surpass — many of the famous old European names. For the wine enthusiast, keeping up with this taste explosion becomes almost a full-time, albeit a pleasurable, occupation.

And now health concerns have been added to the conundrum. In that regard, though, there's good news for North American consumers — and winemakers too. When it comes to those heart-saving antioxidants, French wines from Burgundy and Bordeaux are hard to beat. But before you groan and clutch your wallet (in fact, many French wines, apart from those from Burgundy, are quite reasonably priced), you should know that North America has been blessed with at least two wine regions producing some of the most promising wines in terms of antioxidants, particularly, resveratrol. Those regions: Oregon, in the northwest corner of the United States, and the Niagara region of Ontario, hugging the western end of Lake Ontario.

For those who want to venture further, I'm going to suggest a system to help you pick the wines likeliest to provide protection against coronary heart disease and other illnesses. In addition, I'll list favourably reviewed wines that, while their antioxidant count has not been established, fit the profile for wines containing significant amounts of the vital flavonoids.

The rules are fairly simple, and once you have used them a few times, you will be able to tell at a glance the wines to buy. But please note: wine is not a medicine. If you don't enjoy wine, don't drink it just because you think it will do you good. Also, although I am offering some guidance about wine's healthful qualities, I hope that you won't stick rigidly to drinking only wines that bear "the Jones seal of approval," as it were. You would be denying yourself the pleasure of thousands of wines from around the world, each with something special to offer. Wine is to be enjoyed; only by a great stroke of luck is it also life-preserving.

It's also worth remembering that the arguments over which flavonoids in wine are most beneficial are far from over. It's still a highly controversial subject. The overall importance of wine — and especially red wine — in guarding against coronary heart disease and other illnesses is not likely to be contradicted by future research. But exactly how wine does its heart-saving task will be debated for a long time to come. So, while the information offered here may be useful to you in picking wines, it is not the final word.

You should know first that there are just three main variables when it comes to choosing the best wine from a health viewpoint: the type of grape, the region where the grapes were grown, and the techniques used in making the wine. A fourth — how the wine was stored and transported — is marginal and also hard to monitor.

The comprehensive testing of wines for their health-giving flavonoids is in its infancy. Methods are being improved upon all the time, and the day may soon come when you will be able to pick a wine from the shelf according to a combined antioxidant quotient on the label.

In the meantime, the guidelines that follow resulted from testing by Professor Leroy Creasy at Cornell University; Andrew Waterhouse and his team at the University of California, Davis; and Professor David Goldberg at the University of Toronto, Alex Karumanchiri at the LCBO, and George Soleas at the Canadian Wine Institute. However, I will take responsibility here for any advice offered.

In most cases we have used the presence of resveratrol as the key indicator for antioxidant content. That's not because resveratrol is necessarily the best or only useful flavonoid in wine. And, like the other flavonoids in wine, its actual antioxidant effect in the human body still has to be established by larger-scale clinical trials. But attention focused first on resveratrol because of its presence in ancient eastern folk medicines, and much of the early investigation centred around it. It may be a highly significant flavonoid — only time and more research will tell. For now it's safe to say resveratrol is highly effective in preventing platelet aggregation — and therefore clot formation in the coronary arteries — and in boosting the HDL cholesterol. It is not as effective as an antioxidant as, for instance, quercetin or epicatechin, two other useful flavonoids found in wine, but its content is important for our purposes: the latest Toronto tests, taking in a whole range of flavonoids, show that where the resveratrol count is high counts for the other flavonoids also tend to be high (except in California, whose wines, as we have seen, have a seesaw effect with respect to the presence of resveratrol and quercetin).

"It is a good indicator of thorough skin extraction," says Karumanchiri. The presence of resveratrol means the wine was left in contact with the grape skins long enough for the other flavonoids as well to leach into the wine. We also know that resveratrol is most abundant in cool, damp climates like that of Bordeaux or Oregon, and is found in smaller amounts in grapes grown in hotter climates like those of Italy, Spain, or California. (The following figures graphically show comparisons between countries: the first shows total resveratrol comparisons and the second compares resveratrol types [isomers].)

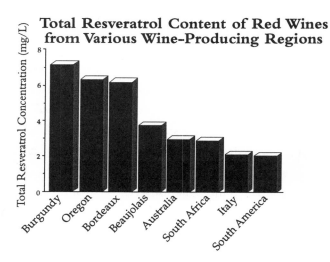

Total Resveratrol Content of Red Wines from Various Wine-Producing Regions

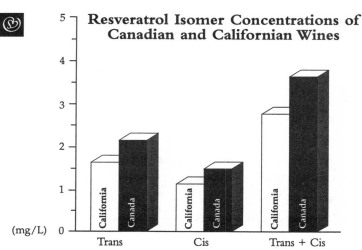

Resveratrol Isomer Concentrations of Canadian and Californian Wines

So the absence of resveratrol doesn't necessarily mean low flavonoid content, because other flavonoids like quercetin and catechin may be present. High resveratrol almost certainly means a wine potentially good for your heart; low resveratrol means you need to take a second look for climate factors.

The first and well nigh immutable rule is that white wines contain very little of the heart-saving flavonoids. I wish it wasn't so. And some day it may be possible to add flavonoids to put white wine on an equal footing with red. The skins of the white grapes from which white wine are made often contain far fewer flavonoids than the skins of red grapes. There are exceptions: the skins of Riesling grapes, for instance, contain significant amounts of resveratrol. But, as we have seen, these measurements are practically meaningless since the grape skins are removed at the start of the fermentation process for white wine. However, alcohol does provide 50 percent of the protection against atherosclerosis — and perhaps more. So a glass or two of white wine will certainly be doing you some good.

It's tempting to believe that, simply by holding the wine up to the light and noting its body and the depth of its ruby colour, you should be able to identify a product high in resveratrol and other flavonoids. It's not so. The opaqueness of the wine is a clue to its strong flavour, but resveratrol and most other flavonoids, says Professor Goldberg, are colourless. In fact, Pinot Noir, the grape that consistently produces wine with the highest resveratrol counts, also produces a wine that is comparatively light in colour with hardly a hint of its potentially powerful ingredients.

When we start talking about regions, especially in France, you might get the impression that it's only expensive wines that may be good for your heart. It's not true. The surprising thing is that it's often the most expensive wines that have the lowest resveratrol content, and for one simple reason. Aging wine in oak barrels — the technique used to produce many top class wines — reduces the resveratrol, sometimes by half. The longer the wine remains in oak, says Goldberg, the greater the loss. Whether other flavonoids are lost in this process is not known. Most wines today are aged in stainless steel tanks.

Wines made using traditional methods (avoiding heavy filtering) — usually at smaller wineries — are quite likely to have higher flavonoid content. It almost goes without saying that mass-produced wine, made with grapes or juice of unknown origin and employing manufacturing shortcuts such as heat-pressing, ending up with the heavy filtering for clarity, is likely to be low or even totally lacking in flavonoid content. Some mass-produced wines are so devoid of ingredients from the original grape that laboratories have a name for them: dead wines.

You're probably best to avoid anything that simply says "red wine." It may be just dandy — but you have no way of knowing what grapes went into the wine, where they came from or how the wine was made.

In the last decade, New World wine producers fought back against the French wine mystique by plainly labelling their wines with the grape type used — Cabernet Sauvignon, for example. Now the French do it too with their "generic" wines. And some of the generics are very good in flavonoid terms. For instance, an inexpensive French 1994 generic, made with Merlot grapes, recently registered one of the highest flavonoid counts ever at the Toronto laboratories. A good generic — made from the right grapes, coming from the right country or region — is a useful staple for your everyday table. You could spend a lot more and be benefitting less. The good grapes to look out for: Pinot Noir, of course, and its offspring, such as Pinotage. Cabernet Sauvignon, in the right climate, is a high resveratrol producer, but variations are large. This climate-sensitive grape, grown in Ontario, may produce two to two and a half times as much resveratrol as grapes of the same species grown in Australia or South Africa, and in France, four times as much. Other grapes that perform well and that tend to be impervious to climate are Merlot, Gamay, and Shiraz.

In reviewing flavonoid content from country to country and region to region, I frequently use some earlier resveratrol counts derived from the Toronto tests. They are for trans-resveratrol, just one form of the substance. Since then, besides cis-resveratrol, two glucosides of resveratrol have been discovered, and there may be more yet. There is much more resveratrol in wine than was earlier believed (although in quantity terms it is still a minor player compared with some other flavonoids). But the original figures, which have been confirmed by the latest tests, are useful as a basis for comparing wines from different regions. And, as mentioned above, a high resveratrol count indicates other flavonoids are likely to be high too.

Bear in mind that the resveratrol figures are for general comparison only. Resveratrol counts vary from season to season and thus from vintage to vintage, and even from one vineyard to the next in the same season. The best plan, from a health point of view, is to drink a variety of wines instead of sticking to one brand or vintage.

I'm also listing below the names of wines from each region. And while I can't give detailed figures on their antioxidant content, these wines come recommended on the basis of quality and price. Because the North American market is so fragmented, I can only offer wine names and approximate prices — you'll have to hunt down sources of supply yourself. In price terms, A indicates inexpensive (usually less than $7); B indicates

$7 to $10; C indicates $10 to $18; and D signifies over $18. Prices refer to Canadian dollars.

My sources, to whom I am most grateful, include Tony Aspler, author of *Vintage Canada* (Toronto: McGraw-Hill Ryerson) and many other excellent wine books; Anthony Rose and Tim Atkin, authors of *Grapevine: The Complete Wine Buyer's Handbook* (London: Headline); and industry wine tasters.

FRANCE

BURGUNDY
Mean trans-resveratrol level, 4.39 milligrams per litre.

The champ, the unbeatable. It's difficult not to score when you buy wines from the boomerang-shaped, famous region running down the centre of France from Chablis to Beaune and down to Lyon. And it's not hard to understand why. Pinot Noir is the grape used universally for red Burgundy, whether it's in the plummier, darker products of the Côte de Nuits or the lighter wines of the Côte de Beaune, the two principal zones in the fabulous Côte d'Or.

In addition to significant antioxidant content, the best of the Pinot Noirs from this region also enjoy another small advantage: aficionados swear they are the sweetest-tempered wines in the world, with a lingering and unforgettable appeal. They use words like "smoke" and "strawberries" and "raspberries" and "violets" in a vain attempt to capture that quality in words.

It would be too much to expect that refinement at bargain basement prices. But, regardless of price (and let's face it, Burgundy prices are never rock bottom), they are likely to rank high in resveratrol content. In total antioxidant content, too — when Professor Tom Whitehead prevailed on the wine waiter at his London club to save samples of some quality French wines for him to test, two Burgundies, a Savigny-lès-Beaune and a Santenay, produced top figures.

In the Toronto tests, wines from Côte de Nuits had a mean resveratrol content of 4.72 — slightly higher than the wines from Côte de Beaune at 3.79. A number of generic or brand name wines from the region scored as well or better than the famous names, with Bourgogne Rouge registering a very respectable 6.51.

Names to consider in the Burgundy region:

Pinot Noir, Boisset,	C
Pinot Noir, Latour,	C
Côte de Beaune-Villages, J. Drouhin,	D
Mâcon Supérieur, Bouchard P. & F.,	C
Nuit-St-Georges, Paul Dugenais,	D
Clos de Chenôves, Bourgogne Rouge, Cave de Buxy,	C
Hautes-Côtes de Beaune, Denis Carré,	C
Gérard Julien, Côte de Nuits-Villages,	D
Givry Clos Marceaux, Laborde-Juillot,	D
Hautes-Côtes de Beaune, Jayer-Gilles,	D
Hautes-Côtes de Nuits, Jayer-Gilles,	D
Savigny-lès-Beaune, Les Guettes, Domaine Pavelot,	D
Vosne-Romanée, Mongeard-Mugneret,	D
Clos de la Féguine, Domaine Jacques Prieur,	D
Château de Rully Rouge,	D
Chorey-lès-Beaune, Tollot Beaut et Fils,	D
Chassagne-Montrachet, Carillon,	D
Santenay, Clos Genet, Denis Philibert,	C
Pinot Noir, Vin de Pays de l'Aude,	B
Santenay Clos Rousseau, Domaine Morey,	D
Chambolle-Musigny, Domaine Machard de Gramont,	D
Gevrey-Chambertin, Domaine Burguet,	D
Bourgogne Rouge, Faiveley,	C
St. Aubin Rouge, Les Combes, Vincent Prunier,	D
Volnay, Louis Jadot,	D
Red Burgundy Pinot Noir, Jean-Claude Boisset,	B

BEAUJOLAIS
Mean trans-resveratrol level, 2.88 milligrams per litre.

Although Beaujolais is part of the Burgundy Region, it is unique in the grapes used — Gamay — and the method employed in making the world famous Beaujolais Nouveau. This is wine for our times — speeded up, whisked to our tables only weeks away from the vine. Instead of being crushed and the juice extracted, the bunches of grapes are initially dumped intact into the vat, in a process called "whole-berry fermentation." The weight of the grapes bursts the skins of those at the bottom, and fermentation starts spontaneously, the top of the vat soon filling with carbon dioxide and expelling oxygen. A few days later, the grapes are lightly crushed and fermentation is completed without the skins.

The whole aim is to avoid the heavy tannins — and therefore many of the flavonoids — so that the wine, ready for drinking in only a month, will have that characteristic light, fruity flavour. Wonderful stuff, but there is a price to pay, of course. The wine does not last, and skin extraction is modest. The Nouveaus, as a result, have a low resveratrol content. Ordinary Beaujolais or Beaujolais Supérieur, often a dark wine that will age for six or seven years, is a different matter. These wines are more in line with their Burgundy cousins and are potentially more heart-sustaining than the Nouveaus. The Gamay grapes of the Beaujolais region, in fact, are often combined with Pinot Noir to produce a wine named Passe-Tout-Grains.

Some wines to consider:

Beaujolais Villages, Duboeuf,	B
Beaujolais Villages, Domaine de St. Ennemond,	C
Beaujolais Villages, Domaine des Ronze,	B
Beaujolais Villages, Bouchacourt,	B

Fleurie Domaine Verpoix,	C
Fleurie Domaine des Quatre Vents, Duboeuf,	D
Bourgogne Passe-Tout-Grains, Jaffelin,	B
Moulin-à-Vent, Tour de Bief, Duboeuf,	C
Regnié, Domaine des Braves, Franck Cinquin,	C

BORDEAUX

Mean trans-resveratrol level, 3.89 milligrams per litre.

The navel of the world in fine-wine terms — far outstripping Burgundy production, its 1,294.9 square kilometres of vineyards constitute the largest fine-wine area in the world, and its châteaux are a byword for some of the best red wines in the world. This is the home of claret, made from a combination of Cabernet Sauvignon, Cabernet Franc, and Merlot grapes, and produced generally on the right bank of Gironde. And now, in health terms too, the Merlot and Cabernet grapes of the Bordeaux region, cooled by the mists and breezes off the Bay of Biscay, set a standard hard to beat.

In the Toronto tests, some of Bordeaux's most famous wines, those from Médoc, as well as the wines of St. Emilion, came out slightly lower than other wines in the region, but that could have been a fluke of the vintage. The pattern was set from the start when, in the first resveratrol tests done several years ago by Leroy Creasy at Cornell, a red Bordeaux scored highest of the twenty-eight French and American wines tested. When Professor Whitehead tested a batch of French wines for total antioxidant content, several Bordeaux products came out well, including Château Moulinet, Château Les Ormes de Pez, Cru Bourgeois, Château Greysac, and, the tops, Château Contemerle.

Old world wine-making methods here are the assurance of maximum skin extraction and minimal tampering with the product before it reaches the palate — and the arteries.

Some names to toy with — and the good news too is that clarets are generally more moderately priced than wines from Burgundy:

Calvet Reserve, Calvet,	C
Château Puyfromage, A. Albert,	C
La Cour Pavillon, Loudenne,	C
Mouton-Cadet Rouge, P. De Rothschild,	C
Sirius, Sichel,	C
St. Emilion, Gabriel Corcol,	B
Margaux, Barton and Guestier,	C
Merlot, Barton and Guestier,	C
St. Julien, Barton and Guestier,	C
Château La Fôret, Bordeaux,	B
Château de Clos Delord, Bordeaux Rouge,	B
Château du Peyrat, Premières Côtes de Bordeaux,	B
Château Lalande d'Auvion, Médoc,	C
Château Fournas Bernadotte, Haut-Médoc,	C
Château Tour-Prignac, Médoc,	C
Château Poujeaux, Moulis-en-Médoc,	D
Château Chasse-Spleen,	D
Château St. Georges, St. Georges St. Emilion,	D
Clos Fourtet, St. Emilion Premier Grand Cru Classé,	D
Château de Francs, Côtes de Francs,	C
Château Lilian Ladouys, St. Estèphe,	D
Château de France, Pessac-Léognan,	C
Château de Parenchère, Bordeaux Supérieur,	C
Château Balac, Haut-Médoc,	C
Château Pierrousselle Rouge, Michel Lafon,	B
Château Beau Site, St. Estèphe,	D
Claret, AC Bordeaux, Cuvée VE,	A
Château La Perrière, Bordeaux, Majestic,	B
Château Cantemerle, Haut-Médoc,	D
Château de Valois, Pomerol,	D
Château Lacousse, Classic Claret,	B
Château Gazin, Pomerol,	D
Château Mingot, Côtes de Castillon,	B

Château les Tonnelles de Fronsac,	B
Château Maine-Bonnet, Graves,	C
Château Lascombes, Margaux,	D
Bertineau St.Vincent, Michel Rolland, Lalande de Pomerol,	D
St. Emilion, Christian Moueix,	C
Margaux, Lucien Lurton,	C
Cabernet Sauvignon, Barton and Guestier,	C

THE RHÔNE VALLEY
Mean trans-resveratrol level, 3.60 milligrams per litre.

Only a whisker behind the Bordeaux wines in resveratrol content, the Rhône wines, including Côtes du Rhône, Côte Rôtie, Châteauneuf-du-Pape, and Hermitage, were remarkably consistent in their good scores, suggesting thorough skin extraction.

The northern Rhône is the home of the Syrah grape, the dark, strongly flavoured berry that has become a mainstay in California and (under the name Shiraz) Australia. Further south, Rhône reds are made using blends of Syrah, Grenache, Cinsault, Mourvèdre, or Carignan grapes.

Some names to think about:

Côtes du Rhône-Villages, Rasteau,	B
La Vieille Ferme, Côtes du Ventoux,	B
Côtes du Rhône, Vidal Fleury,	C
Crozes-Hermitage, Jaboulet,	C
Crozes-Hermitage, Bernard Chave,	C
Château St-Maurice Côtes du Rhône,	B
Château Grand Prebois, Côtes du Rhône,	C
Rasteau La Ramillade, Château du Trignon, Côtes du Rhône Villages,	C
Coudoulet de Beaucastel, Côtes du Rhône,	C
Domaine de Prebayon, Côtes du Rhône Villages,	B

Beaumes-de-Venise, Carte Noire, Côtes du Rhône Villages,	B
Côtes du Rhône, Guigal,	C
Côte Rôtie, Gilles Barge,	D
Côtes du Rhône, Jean-Luc Colombo,	C
Château de la Ramière, Côtes du Rhône,	B
Châteauneuf-du-Pape, Domaine Font de Michelle,	D
Châteauneuf-du-Pape, Les Couversets, J. Quiot,	C
Châteauneuf-du-Pape, Château de Beaucastel,	D
Châteauneuf-du-Pape, Domaine André Brunel,	D
Châteauneuf-du-Pape, Château des Fines Roches, Barrot,	D

A number of tests were conducted on French wines from other regions, with varying results. One consistent theme: Pinot Noir always performed well, with an Alsatian Pinot scoring 7.94, and a Pinot from the Loire Valley a very respectable 10.8. Of the generics tested, Le Piat de Merlot was amongst the highest scorers.

CANADA

Mean trans-resveratrol level, 3.16 milligrams per litre.

A decade or two ago, Ontario wines got no respect. There were some nice Chardonnays and a great deal of inferior sherry catering to the sweet tooth of that era. Drinking Ontario red was considered an act of Canadian patriotism rather than a pleasurable indulgence. Now a lot of that has changed.

In 1988, the Ontario Wine Council set up the Vintners' Quality Alliance (VQA) to encourage the production of superior wines. Not only did 100 percent of the grapes used in VQA wines have to be local and identified on the label, but their ripeness had to be certified, and the wine had to pass a government blind taste test every year before it could be identified as VQA.

As a result, a number of VQA wines, which make up about 20 percent of Ontario production, have won international prizes. More to the point here, because grapes grown in this region are high in resveratrol, and because traditional methods are used in VQA production, these Ontario reds produced some of the highest readings anywhere. The mist that rises from Niagara Falls is an apt symbol for the generally cool, damp climate experienced (not only in the Niagara grape-growing area to the north, but also in the New York State wine region along the south shore of Lake Ontario). This is resveratrol country.

One Ontario VQA product, a blend of Pinot Noir and Cabernet Sauvignon, scored an outstanding 16. British Columbia too has now introduced the VQA scheme with similar results. Many non-VQA wines have respectable antioxidant scores, but the nearest thing you're likely to get to a guarantee of antioxidant correctness is the presence on the label of those three little letters: VQA. As usual, Pinot Noirs were top of the heap. Here are some names to remember among the more inexpensive Pinots from Ontario and British Columbia:

Inniskillin,	B
Pelee Island,	B
Château des Charmes,	B
Gray Monk,	C
Quails' Gate Pinot Noir Reserve,	C
LeComte,	B
Hainle,	C
Stoney Ridge,	B

Ontario Cabernet Sauvignons also yielded high antioxidant counts. Some to watch for:

Château des Charmes,	B
Lakeview Cellars,	B

Stoney Ridge,	B
Peller Estates,	B
Jackson-Triggs,	B
Kittling Ridge,	A

But, as mentioned above, for Canadian consumers concerned about heart health, the best idea is to head for the VQA shelves in your wine or liquor store.

UNITED STATES

OREGON
Mean trans-resveratrol level, 4.3 milligrams per litre.

Oregon is not exactly a household name on the world wine scene, although this promises to change: the region produces superior quality wines. Oregon is poised to take advantage of the new interest in wine's healthful attributes. Next to the wines of Burgundy, the Pinot Noirs of Oregon have the potential to do your heart more good than wines from just about anywhere else in the world.

It was thought rash indeed when, thirty years ago, the pioneer growers of the Willamette Valley in western Oregon planted Pinot Noir, a fussy grape that, at that point, had given growers further south in California nothing but grief. They must have known something: even winemakers in Burgundy, where a lack of sunshine often leaves the Pinot Noir grapes unripe, are showing an interest in Oregon, where longer hours of sunshine do a better job. Robert Drouhin, a well-known name in Burgundy, believes so firmly in Oregon's future that he established a winery in the Dundee Hills and appointed his daughter, Veronique, as winemaker.

With wine production controlled by the strictest laws in the United States and a dedication to quality that is not so apparent among some of the huge California wineries (although there are also plenty of quality wineries in that state), the Oregon producers have found their niche. Now, thanks to their damp, cool climate and the grape they opted for, Oregon winemakers could be big winners in the antioxidant stakes.

Early tests showing high resveratrol levels in Oregon Pinot Noirs, says Alex Karumanchiri, have only been confirmed by newer, much more extensive tests that reveal the wines contain high levels of just about every one of the useful flavonoids.

Some of the names to look out for: Amity, Domaine Drouhin, St. Innocent, Adelsheim, Knudsen-Erath, Bethel Heights, Cameron, Eyrie, Ponzi, Rex Hill, Callahan Ridge, Panther Creek, and Vintage House.

CALIFORNIA
Mean trans-resveratrol level, 1.47 milligrams per litre.

It's the General Motors of the world wine business — with a model to fit every taste and wallet. With more than eight hundred bonded wineries and still growing, the California wine industry dominates the U.S. market; it is a giant hard to ignore. Which explains why, singlehandedly, it has in recent decades swung the world production of wine in a new direction. It was the first to remove a lot of the mystique, not to say snobbery, from wine drinking by clearly labelling the bottle with the name of the grape variety. Consumers soon caught on and realized that, instead of opting for château this or château that, they could buy Cabernet Sauvignon or Merlot and effectively compare similar products whether they came from the Napa Valley or the banks of the Rhône. The California ploy proved so successful that soon everyone was following suit, even the French.

But the God of the Vine, who has smiled so serenely on California, omitted one thing: by no stretch can anyone claim that California wines are well endowed with resveratrol. The state's hot, desert-like climate precludes resveratrol, which thrives where it's cool and damp. Not surprisingly, California's wine experts tend to pooh-pooh the importance of resveratrol, and claim that other antioxidants found in abundance in California reds are more important. Only time and a good deal more research will settle the argument.

Meanwhile, as a consolation, California Pinot Noirs, an increasingly important segment of the California market, are as high there in resveratrol as they are everywhere else. Toronto tests of seven Pinot Noirs from California produced a high mean level of close to 6 milligrams of trans-resveratrol per litre. A Pinot Noir tested at the University of California, Davis, also showed a high count for quercetin, valued as a cancer-fighter as well as an antioxidant. Tests at Davis and Toronto leave no doubt at all that other useful flavonoids are present in significant amounts in the California products.

Several Cabernet Sauvignons tested at Davis showed sub-stantial levels of catechin and epicatechin, both powerful antioxidants, as well as quercetin. A bottle of Petite Sirah (not the same grape variety as Syrah) had the highest amount of cat-echin of any wine tested in Davis, while wines made with Merlot grapes also contained significant amounts of cate-chin and epicatechin. A Zinfandel, made from the lively, dark grape native to California, also had a high catechin content.

The white California wines, the Chardonnays, the Sauvignon Blancs, and the white Zinfandels, contained no quercetin at all, slight traces of resveratrol, and either very small amounts of other flavonoids or none at all.

When the California investigators put the phenolics to the test in preventing oxidation of LDL cholesterol, the red wine flavonoids were 46 percent to a phenomenal 100 per-cent effective. The white wine flavonoids achieved only a

3 to 6 percent success rate.

Much more testing needs to be done — not only to establish the amount of flavonoids in wine, but also to show precisely how effective they are in throwing a block tackle at coronary heart disease.

Some California Pinot Noirs to add to your list:

Acacia,	D
Pedroncelli,	C
Parducci,	C
Robert Mondavi Reserve,	D
Saintsbury Carneros,	D
Saintsbury Garnet,	D
Los Carneros, Carneros Creek,	D
Fleur de Carneros, Carneros Creek,	D
Calera Central Coast,	D
Mirssou Harvest Reserve,	D
Paul Masson,	C
Monterey Classic Pinot Noir,	B

Some other names to consider:

Glen Ellen Merlot, Proprietor's Reserve,	B
Sutter Home Zinfandel,	B
Fetzer Eagle Point Petite Sirah,	C
Zinfandel, Cartlidge & Brown,	B
Robert Mondavi Pinot Noir, Napa Valley,	D
Sutter Home Merlot,	B
Ravenswood Zinfandel,	C
Rosenblum Zinfandel,	C

NEW YORK

New York's strength, like Oregon's, lies in its Pinot Noirs. Historically, New York growers, whose production is only second in the United States to that of California, relied on North American grape species, but in recent years they have turned increasingly to the vinefera — the classic European grapes. Of these, Pinot Noirs have found a home that suits them around the Finger Lakes wine region, while Long Island growers — almost within sight of New York City — have specialized in Merlots and Cabernet Sauvignons. It's a switch in species that could pay off for New York growers, as customers become aware of the relative health potential of wines made with these grapes.

The New York industry is also lucky in having Professor Leroy Creasy, the United States's biggest drum beater for resveratrol, working nearby at Cornell University. Creasy has drawn the world's attention to the high resveratrol content of many New York wines, particularly the Pinot Noirs. Although we don't have figures to compare resveratrol content with that of wines from France, Oregon, and elsewhere, Creasy told me that one Pinot Noir he had recently checked showed the highest level of any wine he has tested, including those from France.

Some New York wines (all in the C category) for your list:

Dr. Konstantin Frank's Pinot Noir
Bedell Cellars Merlot
Lenz Winery Merlot
Millbrook Merlot
Arcadian Estate Pinot Noir
Brotherhood Pinot Noir
Glenora Merlot
Lamoreux Landing Pinot Noir
McGregor Pinot Noir
NewLand Pinot Noir
Pindar Pinot Noir
Gristina Merlot
Hermann J. Weimer Pinot Noir

Lakewood Pinot Noir
Palmer Merlot
Peconic Bay Merlot
Wagner Pinot Noir
Palmer Cabernet Sauvignon

AUSTRALIA

Mean trans-resveratrol level, 1.47 milligrams per litre.

Australian wines are friendly, easy to like, and often good value. If you're new to the wine game, a bottle of Koonunga Hill Shiraz–Cabernet Sauvignon or Wolf Blass Yellow Label Cabernet Sauvignon is a lively wake-up call for the taste buds. Full-fruit-flavoured, inclined to be oaky, many Australian products make up in cheerful amiability what some experts may feel they lack in subtlety.

In antioxidant terms, Shiraz seems to be the operative word in Australia. In the tests, wines made with Shiraz (or Syrah) grapes scored consistently higher than Cabernet Sauvignon or Cabernet–Shiraz blends. Again, however, if you can locate an Australian Pinot Noir you are on to a good thing: one Australian Pinot scored an exceptional 13.4.

If resveratrol emerges as the most significant or one of the most significant flavonoids, Australia's best hope may be represented by new vineyards in cooler areas that have been planted with Cabernet, Merlot, and Pinot. We await developments.

Some names to remember:

Remnano Shiraz,	C
Ridoch Limited Release Shiraz,	C
St. Hallett Barossa Shiraz,	C
David Wynn Patriarch Shiraz,	D
Lindeman's Bin 50 Shiraz,	B
Basedow Shiraz,	C

Riddoch Shiraz,	C
Leasingham Shiraz, Clare Valley,	C
Peter Lehmann Vine Vale Shiraz,	B
Craigmoor Mudgee Shiraz,	C
Jamieson's Run Coonawarra,	C
E & E Black Pepper Shiraz,	D
Penfolds Bin 2, Shiraz/Mourvedre,	B
Rothbury Estate Shiraz, South Eastern Australia,	C
Château Reynella Basket Pressed Shiraz, McLaren Vale,	C
Rockford Basket Press Shiraz,	D
Wolf Blass Shiraz, President's Selection,	D
Mount Langhi Ghiran Shiraz,	C
Wynn's Shiraz, Coonawarra,	C
Yarra Yering Underhill Shiraz,	D
Wynn's St. Michael Hermitage,	D
Wildflower Ridge Shiraz, Western Australia,	B
Hardy's Barossa Valley Shiraz,	C
Rosemount Estate Shiraz,	B
McWilliams Mount Pleasant Philip Shiraz, Hunter River Valley,	C

NEW ZEALAND

Not long ago New Zealand was famous for its superb white wines, especially the Sauvignon Blancs and Chardonnays. And that was it. Today its reds, including Pinot Noirs, Cabernet Sauvignons, and Merlots, are winning attention and prizes. And because they are grown in exactly the kind of cool climates that produce high resveratrol figures everywhere from chilly upstate New York to damp Burgundy, the New Zealand reds bear watching as health becomes the new wine factor.

Some names to watch for:

Waimarama Estate Hawkes Bay Cabernet/Merlot,	D
Montana Cabernet Sauvignon,	B
Corbans Private Bin Cabernet/Merlot,	C

Corbans Merlot,   C
Coopers Creek Huapai Cabernet/Merlot,   C

Some New Zealand Pinot Noirs to watch for: Babich, Corbans, Kumeu River, Matua Marlborough, St. Helena, Vidal, and Villa Maria Estate.

ITALY

Mean trans-resveratrol level, 1.76 milligrams per litre.

Many Italian wines are superb, and yet there are difficulties when it comes to categorizing them on a health basis. Coronary heart disease in Italy is amongst the lowest in the world. Even allowing for the healthful Mediterranean diet, this suggests that Italian wines, which are consumed plentifully, are helping to stave off heart disease. But our resveratrol measurement doesn't work as well here because, with its hot climate, Italy, like California, produces grapes low in trans-resveratrol.

Glucosides of resveratrol (resveratrol attached to sugar) are present in Italian reds, although up to now it is not known if resveratrol in this form finds its way into the blood system. In addition, many of the grape species grown are not the familiar ones, and Italian producers have not traditionally identified grape types on the label — although that is changing.

That said, wines from the Tuscany region did somewhat better in the tests than those from Veneto or Piedmont. Where wine is made exclusively with Cabernet Sauvignon grapes, resveratrol levels are respectable. And Italy may hold out some surprises. Researcher Dr. Fulvio Mattivi has measured up to 7.17 milligrams per litre of trans-resveratrol in red wines from the Trentino region. Cabernet Sauvignon wines were tops, their figures ranging from 1.33 to 7.17, Merlot was next (3.14 to 6.03), with Pinot Noir uncharacteristically third (3.22 to 5.93).

And finally, let's not forget Chianti, the hearty pasta-loving wine of the countryside. Five different grape varieties may be used in making Chianti, including some white grapes. In spite of its raw energy in flavour and colour terms, Chianti does not contain high levels of resveratrol and trails behind the wines mentioned above.

Some Italian suggestions:

Cabernet Sauvignon, Casarsa,	B
Cabernet Sauvignon, La Stoppa,	D
Cabernet Sauvignon, Folonari,	B
Pinot Nero Il Bosco, Zonin,	B
Merlot, Casarsa,	B
Merlot, Collavini,	B
Merlot del Piave Donini,	B
Merlot, Trentino, Ca'vit,	B
Casale del Giglio Shiraz, Vino da Tavola del Lazio,	B
Merlot Grave del Friuli,	A
Merlot/Cabernet Sauvignon Fiordaliso, Vino da Tavola,	B
Merlot del Veneto, Via Nova,	B

SPAIN AND PORTUGAL

Mean trans-resveratrol level, 1.64 milligrams per litre.

Similar difficulties here to the Italian situation. Twenty-six Spanish wines were tested, but they could not be classified by grape of origin. Again, glucosides of resveratrol were present, significantly in Rioja, from Spain's preeminent table wine area in the cooler north of the country. Rioja (Ree-o-ha) is a pleasant wine that smells like strawberries and sandalwood.

Port, the fortified wine from Portugal, is an interesting situation. While sherry does not appear to contain much in the way of antioxidants, port, which is made by partly fermenting the grapes and then stopping the process by adding brandy, does contain glucosides of resveratrol. They may not be significant when you consider that not many people would consume enough port for it to make a health difference.

Here are some Rioja names to remember:

Rioja Campo Viejo Reserva,	C
Rioja Cumbrero Tinto,	B
Rioja Marques De Riscal,	C
Rioja Montelorca,	B
Rioja Vina Monty Gran Reserva,	C
CVNE, Viña Real Rioja,	A
Rioja Crianza Campillo,	B
Contino, Rioja Reserva,	D
Tempranillo Oak-Aged, Rioja Berberana,	B
Campillo Gran Reserva Rioja,	D
Conde de Valdemar Rioja Reserva,	C
Baron de Ley Rioja Reserva,	C

SOUTH AFRICA

South Africa presents one of the most interesting stories in terms of what its wines can, or can't, do for our hearts. With its hot climate, theoretically it really has no business making claims. Yet, in total resveratrol terms, it stands alongside Australia, and well ahead of Italy and Spain. The likely explanation: the Pinotage grape.

In the 1900s, according to wine writer Tony Aspler, Professor Abraham Izak Perold, head of viticulture and enology at Stellenbosch University, snooped around France looking for useful ideas. He learned that Hermitage wine, from the Rhône region, was often used to beef up poor Pinot Noir vintages in Burgundy. The grape used to make Hermitage is our old friend, the Syrah. There was a similar grape familiar in South Africa, called the Cinsaut (spelt slightly differently to the Cinsault of Europe). Professor Perold must have brooded on this observation throughout the First World War; it was not until 1924 that he attempted to cross the Pinot Noir with the workhorse Cinsaut in a plot beside his house on the university campus. Neglected, almost forgotten, it wasn't until 1932 that a student, Christian Theron, discovered the three surviving cross seedlings, and successfully grafted one of them from which all of South Africa's 2,500 hectares of Pinotage have sprung today.

Although the Pinotage grape is South Africa's great wine success story of recent times, that wasn't the way it looked earlier on. The grape was not grown commercially until 1951. Wines made with Pinotage grapes soon started collecting prizes, but even then conservative Boer grape growers were sceptical. It has such a powerful flavour that it tends to overpower any other grape with which it is blended. It didn't have the class, they felt, of a Cabernet Sauvignon or a Merlot. After several ups and downs in popularity, Pinotage has finally come into its own. It produces a powerfully dark purplish wine with a rich aroma and flavour worthy of its Burgundy ancestor. And if breeding counts for anything, the Pinot Noir in its parentage contributes to a healthy resveratrol count.

Some South African wines to consider:

Backsberg Pinotage,	B
Saxenburg Merlot, Stellenbosch,	C
Capelands Merlot,	C
Bellingham Pinotage,	B
Paarl Pinotage,	B
Meerendal Pinotage,	C
Kleindal Pinotage, Vinimark, Robertson,	B
Table Mountain Pinot Noir,	B
Kanonkop Pinotage,	C
Neetlingshof Pinotage,	C

The following were also rated top Pinotages by Tony Aspler

during a 1995 tour of the South African vineyards. They are worth watching for, although I have no information on likely prices: Cathedral Cellars; Clos Malverne; Diemersdal; Groot Constantia; Jacobsdal; Middelvlei; Saxenburg; Simonsig; Eesterivier; Lanzerac; Vlottenburg.

CHILE

The full-bodied and flavoursome reds of Chile have been one of the great discoveries made in the wine world in the last few years. You find them everywhere, valued for their quality as well as their moderate price. And although we may have trouble pronouncing their names, the grapes that go into them are familiar enough — Cabernet Sauvignon, Pinot Noir, Merlot, and Malbec. So it's a shame to have to report that these, along with wines from Argentina, did not perform well when tested for resveratrol. The South American products, most made from Cabernet Sauvignon grapes, ranged from 0.54 milligrams per litre to 4.95. One Merlot from Chile, where wine has been made since the sixteenth century, was outstanding, and Pinot Noirs, as usual, scored well. Personally, I wouldn't let a low resveratrol count stand between me and my Chilean favourites — good news about their antioxidant content could arrive any day.

Some names to occupy us while we wait:

Santa Carolina Merlot,	B
Cono Sur Pinot Noir,	B
Cono Sur Pinot Noir Reserve,	C
Carmen Merlot Reserve,	B
Errazuriz Merlot,	B
Montes Merlot,	B
Concha Y Toro Merlot,	B
Cousino Macul Merlot,	C

San Pedro Merlot,	B
Santa Rita Merlot,	C
Tocornal Pinot Noir,	B

CENTRAL EUROPE

Mean trans-resveratrol level, 3.26 milligrams per litre.

The wines tested here were from Hungary, Bulgaria, and Slovakia and were made from Cabernet Sauvignon, Merlot, Cinsault, and Zweigelt grapes. Wines from Hungary and Bulgaria performed particularly well. Romania is a major producer of Pinot Noir.

Some wines worth noting:

BULGARIA

Burgas Country Red Cabarnet Merlot,	A
Lovico Suhindol Merlot Reserve,	B
Bulgarian Merlot, Haskovo Region,	B
Lyaskovets Reserve Merlot,	B
Bulgarian Reserve Merlot, Lovico Suhindol Region,	A
Bulgarian Stambolovo Special Reserve Merlot,	B
Bulgarian Vintage Premiere Merlot, Iambol Region,	A
Bulgarian Country Wine, Merlot/Pinot Noir, Sliven,	A
Oriachovitza Barrel-Aged Merlot Vintage Premiere,	A
Merlot Reserve Sophia,	A

ROMANIA

Romanian Country Red Pinot Noir/Merlot,	A
Simburesti Pinot Noir,	A
Rovinex Pinot Noir,	A
Premiat Merlot,	A

HUNGARY

Hungarian Merlot, Hungarian Country Wine,	A
Chapel Hill Merlot,	A
St. Stephen's Merlot, Hungarovin,	A
Pinot Noir, Hungarovin,	A

SWITZERLAND

Although Swiss wines make little impact on the North American market — those canny Swiss drink nearly all their excellent products without letting the rest of the world in on the secret — the Pinot Noir grapes grown on that country's mountainous slopes are every bit as rich in resveratrol as those grown in Oregon. Six wines from Switzerland came in with figures ranging from 5.0 to 12.3 milligrams per litre. It's worth bearing in mind on your next skiing or hiking holiday in the Swiss Alps.

CHAPTER VI

A Little Wine for Thine Infirmities

STROKE:
A MEASURE OF PROTECTION

To understand the story on drinking and stroke, it helps to imagine one of those little weather houses where, depending on the forecast, either a smiling woman with a basket of flowers or a man with an umbrella emerges. For the house, read stroke, which is the third-biggest killer in North America (behind heart disease and cancer). For the little man and woman, read alcohol studies. Sometimes the forecast is good and sometimes it's bad. Happily, though, for those who drink moderately, we see more of the smiling woman than we do of the chap with the umbrella.

A stroke occurs when the brain is deprived of the flow of blood and oxygen it requires. This can happen for various reasons, for instance, when one of the arteries leading to the brain becomes clogged, or when a blood vessel bursts, causing bleeding into the brain. Deprived of oxygen, nerve cells die within minutes, causing the partial paralysis, speech impairment, and other unfortunate consequences with which most of us are only too familiar. Strokes caused by clots that block the arteries are called ischemic strokes, and they are by far the most common type, accounting for 70 to 80 percent of strokes. They are kissing cousins to coronary heart disease: in both cases, clots result from the gradual clogging of the arteries — atherosclerosis.

In heart disease, the clot occurs in the coronary artery, hits the heart, and impairs its function; in an ischemic stroke, the clot occurs in an artery bringing blood to the brain (cerebral thrombosis). There's a second, less common type of stroke called a cerebral embolism that involves a wandering clot. It starts out elsewhere in the body, usually in the heart, and makes its way to the brain where it does its damage.

The other two types of stroke, which you could compare with your pipes bursting and flooding the house, are called hemorrhagic strokes. The subarachnoid hemorrhage, accounting for 7 percent of all strokes, occurs when a blood vessel on the surface of the brain ruptures, allowing blood to seep between the brain and the skull. A cerebral hemorrhage, on the other hand, involves a rupture right down inside the brain and can be caused by a bash to the head or an aneurism — a swollen weak point in the artery wall — bursting. It accounts for 10 percent of strokes.

The hemorrhagic stroke — the burst pipe — is the one to fear most: pressure on the brain from the internal bleeding causes death in 50 percent of cases. Although, if you survive, recovery is faster than if you have had a clot-caused stroke. That may sound rather complicated, but when it comes to the effect alcohol has on strokes, it's all really rather simple.

Remember how moderate alcohol consumption helped protect against coronary heart disease by boosting the HDL cholesterol and reducing the platelet aggregation that led to clotting? The same effect, many scientists believe, works against ischemic or clot-caused strokes, which are by far the commonest sort. If free-flowing blood, unlikely to clog, is helpful to the heart, it can be equally helpful in preventing a clot reaching the brain. On the other hand, the last thing you need in the case of a hemorrhage in the brain is blood that won't clot. It means the leakage will continue and the damage will be worse. So the very thing that was good in preventing an ischemic stroke is potentially bad in the case of a hemorrhagic stroke.

Even a couple of hundred years ago, doctors observed that heavy drinkers were more likely to die of stroke, and that knowledge has tended to colour much of the research on the subject until recent years. There's no doubt about the danger from heavy drinking: the newest surveys show that if you are a heavy drinker you are about three times as likely to suffer a hemorrhagic stroke compared with a nondrinker. It's not hard to understand why. Heavy drinking increases the blood pressure. Just think of pumping a lot more water through the pipes in that old house of yours, and imagine what it does when it finds a weak spot.

Hypertension, or high blood pressure, is the single greatest risk factor for stroke. Because it is harder to separate out the different types of stroke, especially in the case of death, which would require autopsy, the survey results on light drinking and stroke have not been as clear-cut as those on coronary heart disease. But there are now chinks of light. A Birmingham, England, hospital team, comparing 230 stroke victims with other patients, found in 1986 that people who had just over a drink a day were 50 percent less likely to have a stroke. When their figures were challenged, they made much wider comparisons — and still came to the same conclusion.

Dr. Arthur Klatsky, the cardiologist in Oakland, California, reported in 1989 that people who consumed one or two drinks a day were 25 percent less likely to end up in hospital with a hemorrhagic stroke than abstainers. But if you drank three drinks or more, the odds swung against you, and you were about 40 percent more likely to have a stroke than an abstainer.

Klatsky found the most dramatic benefit with ischemic or clot-caused stroke: light drinkers reduced their risk by 60 percent, while even those drinking three or more drinks a day still got a 50 percent benefit. Klatsky warned, however, that too much shouldn't be read into one study. But the evidence has continued to accrue, notably the Danish study suggesting those who drink three to five glasses of wine a day are 60 percent less likely to die of a stroke.

Dr. Carlos A. Camargo of Brigham and Women's Hospital in Boston, one of the leading world experts in this area, told me that the U.S. Nurses Health Study, which involved 87,000 nurses, showed a reduction in ischemic strokes for nurses consuming one drink a day or less, but an increase in hemorrhagic stroke even with moderate drinking. An American Cancer Society study of 250,000 subjects, on the other hand, showed a reduction in the total stroke count with light drinking. "There's very little evidence that moderate drinking has an adverse effect on total stroke counts," he said. "In terms of beverage type, there is some evidence that red wine may be very beneficial."

Studies in Bordeaux — where else? — suggest that one or two glasses of wine a day reduce the chances of having an ischemic stroke, although how much more effectively than other alcoholic drinks is not clear. Curiously, in scanning the world literature on the subject, Dr. Camargo finds that the Japanese are unique in not seeming to derive any protective benefit from moderate alcohol consumption in the matter of strokes. Another anomaly: African Americans, Asian-Pacific islanders, and Hispanics all experience a higher number of strokes than white populations. The familiar U- or J-shaped profile seems, in fact, to apply mainly to white populations in the case of strokes.

So what should you do? The evidence is not yet decisive enough to suggest that light drinking helps protect you against any sort of stroke. It might be protective against ischemic stroke, and because you are four times as likely to get that type of stroke, the odds are rather in your favour. If you are drinking modest amounts for protection against coronary heart disease, there is probably no reason to fear you are increasing your chances of having a stroke. What the stroke and alcohol studies do show decisively is that there is a terrific risk in drinking too much, emphasizing once again that the health benefits that come from drinking wine or other alcoholic beverages are related to moderate drinking only.

What are the other risk factors for stroke? There are some you can't avoid, like growing old, being male, and having a family history of stroke. Cigarette smoking, as always, is a risk, but with a special rider here: women who smoke and are on the birth control pill increase their chances of stroke significantly. Heart disease, surprisingly, is a risk factor too — if you have the one you are more likely to get the other. So all the risk factors for coronary heart disease — high cholesterol, high blood pressure, and so on, apply equally to stroke. If you ask, what can I do to avoid having a stroke, the first and obvious answer is to have your blood pressure checked regularly and get it under control if necessary. Eating a healthful diet and exercising may even be enough to do the trick. Be aware too of the warning signs of stroke:

℃ Any sudden dimness or loss of vision, especially in one eye.

℃ Loss of speech or trouble understanding people.

℃ Sudden weakness or numbness of the face, arm or leg, or one side of the body.

℃ Sudden dizziness or even an unexplained fall.

℃ Sudden piercing headaches with no known cause.

You should also know that about 10 percent of strokes are preceded by "little strokes" — like tremors before an earthquake. These little warnings, which typically last about a minute, are caused by a blood clot that results in a temporary blockage in an artery leading to the brain. The symptoms are similar to those of a full-blown stroke. And, as with stroke symptoms, there is only one thing to do: get to a doctor or hospital as quickly as you can.

KEEP THAT PRESSURE DOWN

Hypertension — high blood pressure — is the dangerous little secret one person in four carries around with them in Canada and the United States. Dangerous because nothing is a surer indicator of a potential heart attack or stroke. Hypertension is the fire alarm, the warning rocket, the yellow flag that Nature uses to say "trouble ahead." When blood pressure goes up, the body is signalling frantically that care needs to be taken. But half the time no one's listening.

A 1990 survey of more than twenty thousand people across Canada revealed that more than 33 percent of men with hypertension and 15 percent of women with the condition weren't even aware of it. Blood pressure goes up as we get older, but younger people can get it too. And there the figures — for men anyway — are worse. Among those in the eighteen to thirty-four age group with hypertension, 57 percent of men weren't even aware of it. The figure for women, who perhaps pay more attention to their health, was a lot better — 14 percent.

But here's the real shocker: of all the people who knew they suffered from hypertension, 59 percent weren't getting any treatment. And a sizeable proportion also came under the heading of "treated but uncontrolled," which often means they're not following their doctor's diet advice or taking their pills.

The Canadian picture is not unique. Studies in the United States, Britain, Australia, and other developed countries have come up with similar findings. What makes these results so frustrating for the medical profession is that high blood pressure, unlike many of the factors that contribute to cardiovascular diseases, is almost completely treatable. The standard instructions for those with hypertension are to cut down on salt, reduce weight, start exercising, and reduce excessive drinking. The doc may also put you on any one of a whole range of blood pressure–lowering medications.

The trick, then — because hypertension has no symptoms — is to keep taking your medication without fail. Don't be like my dear and still very much missed mother-in-law: she only took her hypertension pills when she happened to remember. And she died of an aneurism. Why it's of special concern to us here is that, after obesity, excessive alcohol consumption is one of the major contributing factors to high blood pressure. It's estimated that 7 to 11 percent of male hypertension is due to drinking too much. In women the figure is much lower because women tend to drink a lot less.

The first scientist to rumble to the alcohol-hypertension connection was a French physician, Dr. Camille Lian. During the First World War, he measured the blood pressures of soldiers who were "moderate" drinkers (up to 2 litres of wine a day), heavy drinkers (2 to 3 litres), and very heavy drinkers (over 3 litres). After drinking all that, hypertension, you would think, would have been the least of the soldiers' problems! Dr. Lian found that the heaviest drinkers were much more prone to hypertension.

What causes high blood pressure? In addition to age, salt, obesity, and too much alcohol, hereditary factors, hardening of the arteries (atherosclerosis), and contraction of the tiny blood vessels (the arterioles) all make their contribution. But when you get right down to it, doctors admit that most of the time they have no idea of the actual cause. Its effects, though, are pretty drastic. The heart has to pump that much harder to force the blood around the body, putting itself and the arteries under greater strain. The result is that the heart can become enlarged and the arteries are likely to be damaged from the hammering they're taking. Not a pretty picture.

In a book extolling the health benefits of wine, the critical question here is: how much alcohol is too much in terms of causing hypertension? There have been dozens of studies around the world, and they don't all agree. The ubiquitous Dr. Arthur Klatsky, as long ago as 1977, discovered the familiar U- or J-shaped curve for hypertension among women drinkers, although not among men. In other words, women who drank moderately were at slightly less risk for hypertension than women who either didn't drink at all or drank heavily.

Some studies in Germany, New Zealand, and Australia have also come up with J- or U-shaped profiles. But the evidence that light drinking actually modestly reduces blood pressure isn't nearly as strong as that confirming the positive benefits that moderate drinking has in reducing coronary artery disease. So the research tends to focus on finding the drinking threshold beyond which blood pressure climbs significantly.

Reviewing the evidence at a conference in Toronto in December 1994, Dr. Klatsky said one or two standard drinks a day only causes a slight increase in the blood pressure. And the danger zone? An international survey done in 1993 put the danger zone — beyond which blood pressure rises significantly — at anything above 30 grams of alcohol a day — about 2.5 standard drinks.

A British government cardiovascular review group came up with a very similar finding regarding blood pressure. It put the danger threshold at four British units per day — again, about

2.5 drinks. Dealing with the choice of alcoholic beverage, Dr. Klatsky told his audience that the increase in diastolic pressure (between heartbeats) was the same for wine, beer, and spirits. But systolic pressure (taken when the heart beats) was highest for spirits, lower for beer, and lowest for wine. "There may be a built-in benefit in wine," he said, but he added his usual rider: in North America, wine drinkers tend to be healthier and wealthier than consumers of beer and spirits. "People who pick wine," he said, "tend to be women, tend to be temperate, tend to smoke much less, are much better educated, and have fewer symptoms." Dr. Klatsky endorsed a recommendation of the U.S. National High Blood Pressure Education Reporting Group that people not take more than two drinks per day. A patient with hypertension who is having three or more drinks a day should be advised to cut down or abstain, he suggested.

Is it worth the risk at all? The protection you get from heart disease through light or moderate drinking, he said, "far outweighs the possible slight increased risk with regard to hypertension."

CANCER:
BELIEVING THE IMPOSSIBLE

It was a misty, cool winter day in the Napa Valley, and the group with which I was touring the famous Robert Mondavi Winery was huddled in sweaters and coats. Our guide was a tall, rangy man named Peter Dahl who, in his black Western hat, bore a passing resemblance to Gary Cooper. After visiting the little Mondavi family museum in the white, Mission-style winery, after seeing the grapes being processed and examining the expensive French oak barrels in which the wine is aged, we were anticipating the climax of the tour — the tasting.

It was not a disappointment. Peter threw open an oak door and all our faces lit up at the sight of a cheery log fire on that grey day with, to one side, a table set with Mondavi's finest products. The surprise came when, with everyone inside, he closed the door. On the rear, as required by law in California, was a large sign: "Warning: Drinking distilled spirits, beers, coolers, and other alcoholic beverages may increase cancer risk and, during pregnancy, cause birth defects."

We were seeing one result of what has come to be called the "neo-prohibitionist" movement in the United States. The neo-prohibitionists are a potent force made up of religious fundamentalists, people with concerns like Mothers Against Drunk Drivers, old-fashioned moralists fighting under the shield of science (the Center for Science in the Public Interest, for example), and bureaucrats who have made careers from warning people of the dangers of alcohol, real and imagined.

By now Peter Dahl was pouring us small samples of a rather fine Chardonnay from an elegant bottle with a turned lip, just like the bottles from centuries past. Its beauty was somewhat compromised by the extensive warnings the winery, by law, must carry on the label: "Government warning: (1) According to the Surgeon General, women should not drink alcoholic beverages during pregnancy because of the risk of birth defects. (2) Consumption of alcoholic beverages impairs your ability to drive a car or operate machinery, and may cause health problems. Contains sulfites."

Europeans visiting Canada and especially the United States are appalled and amazed at the puritanical attitude towards drinking. The U.S. government's warnings on wine bottles, after all, are attached not to some pharmaceutical wonder drug discovered just yesterday, but to a drink that has comforted the human race for five thousand years or more without apparent ill effects — *when taken in moderation.*

The Europeans shouldn't be too amazed. The European office of the World Health Organization (WHO) based in Geneva has demonstrated a similar mind-set. And on both sides of the Atlantic, cancer fears, largely ungrounded, have been used as a scare tactic to stop people consuming even moderate amounts of wine or other alcoholic drinks.

In California a great new democratic principle has been established: scientific truth is determined not by conscientious examination of the evidence by leading experts in the field, but by a vote of the people. Under the terms of Proposition 65, the people of California have declared that alcohol is carcinogenic — in other words, cancer-causing. In 1987, the International Agency for Research on Cancer (IARC), part of WHO, declared, "The consumption of alcoholic beverages is causally related to the occurrence of cancers of the oral cavity [the mouth], pharynx [throat], larynx [voice box], esophagus and liver." In fairness, it added that these cancers tended to be rare.

So what are the facts? "Ethanol [alcohol] is not a carcinogen by standard laboratory tests," reports Sir Richard Doll and colleagues from Oxford, Switzerland, and the Netherlands in a 1993 review of the evidence on alcohol and cancers of the digestive tract. Dr. Emanuel Rubin, chairman of pathology and cell biology at Jefferson Medical College in Philadelphia, has thrown scorn on the IARC finding. The research on which it was based is "inconsistent and limited," he said, and animal studies have not supported the finding.

Laboratory animals, said Dr. Rubin, a leading expert in the field, have been given the human equivalent of four bottles of whisky a day for their whole lives — without ever developing cancer. Nearly all carcinogens, he said, are mutagens, which means they cause mutation or breaking down in the DNA — the life code. In every test performed, alcohol is not mutagenic, said Dr. Rubin.

Could it be a cancer promoter? Some cells, like the burglar's helper who gives him a boost over the wall, may not be the arch-villains, but certainly help — in this case by stimulating the proliferation of cancer cells and fixing the mutation. According to Dr. Rubin, "it is unlikely to be a promoter."

But here's a mystery: very heavy drinkers are more likely to get cancer of the digestive tract — especially of the esophagus, the muscular tube connecting the throat to the stomach. What's causing it, if not alcohol? Dr. Rubin tentatively points to smoking. Studies show that heavy drinkers tend to smoke a lot. It's almost impossible to separate out the effects of heavy smoking and drinking in men or women — because they nearly always go hand in hand. All that can be said is that heavy alcohol consumption and cigarette smoking act as multipliers on each other.

John Duffy, statistician with the Alcohol Research Group at Edinburgh University, links 45 percent of cancers of the larynx and oral cavity and 35 percent of liver cancers to alcohol. One explanation is the same as above. Heavy drinking is usually linked with smoking, and it is hard to separate the effects of the two. It should also be added that these cancers, though tragic for the individuals involved, do not occur as frequently as other types of cancer. Oral cancers, for example, will account for 1,080 deaths in Canada in 1995, compared to 16,800 lung-cancer deaths.

For nonsmokers, according to the Doll study, the risk is small, "unless consumption [of alcohol] is exceptionally heavy." The scientists add that even then, the risk may be reduced by a diet rich in fruit and green vegetables. It would be a first: "Another double Scotch, bartender, with broccoli on the side!"

There is a geographical curiosity when it comes to cancer — an esophageal cancer belt runs right across Asia from the Caspian Sea to Northern China where rates are often one hundred times those found in Europe. High incidence is found in some villages in Northern Iraq where the population neither smokes nor drinks. Chinese scientists discovered that people in those relatively cold regions dry leafy vegetables for use in winter. When the leaves are soaked in water to ready them for eating, they produce NDMNA, a powerful carcinogenic chemical.

In heavy drinkers, though, Dr. Rubin says cancer of the esophagus may be caused by gastric reflux, which is the regurgitation of the food and stomach juices into the lower esophagus. Alcohol has also been blamed for causing cancer of the liver. That argument, said Dr. Rubin, has now been settled. Heavy alcohol consumption leads to cirrhosis of the liver in a minority of cases, and cirrhosis, on rare occasions, causes liver cancer. Once again the message is that drinking excessively is dangerous to your health and could cost you your life.

But what about moderate drinking and cancer? There the evidence is more encouraging. The 1990 American Cancer Society study that focused on 250,000 subjects found that those drinking one drink a day or less actually reduced their chances of getting cancer by about 10 percent. Again it's a question for the individual of balancing risks. Heavy alcohol consumption, according to a 1981 study by Sir Richard Doll and another researcher, was a contributing factor in 3 percent of American cancer deaths — the same exactly as "geophysical factors" like living at a high altitude. On the other hand, cardiovascular disease, against which moderate alcohol consumption is an important weapon, carries off 76,000

Canadians a year and nearly a million Americans.

BREAST CANCER: AN OPEN QUESTION

In 1987 the *New England Journal of Medicine* came out with a shocker. Not one, but two studies published in the journal linked breast cancer with the consumption of alcohol. A study by the National Cancer Institute suggested that even moderate female drinkers ran a 50 to 100 percent increased risk of getting breast cancer. The second report, from Dr. Walter Willett and colleagues at the Harvard School of Medicine, covered nearly one hundred thousand nurses whose diet and alcohol consumption had been tracked for a number of years. The results: a slightly elevated risk of breast cancer for women who had a drink of beer or spirits every day, and no increase for women who had a glass of wine. (In fairness, Dr. Willett reported in 1993, in a less precise study of Spanish women with breast cancer, that he had found a similar elevated risk, this time with wine.)

The journal reports, and an accompanying editorial, caused a wave of interest among doctors — and concern among women drinkers. If the finding was true, it was of real significance. While cancers of the digestive tract linked to heavy alcohol consumption are rare, breast cancer is one of the two most common forms of cancer (along with lung cancer) among women in the developed countries. There was a rush of research, but answers proved hard to come by. There have now been more than fifty epidemiological studies and there is still no conclusive confirmation.

Part of the problem is that cancer — and breast cancer particularly — has been linked to just about every cause under the sun. Some of the well-known risk factors include having a family history of breast cancer, being single, having your first period early, having your first child at a later age or not having children at all, deciding not to breast-feed, entering menopause late, and having a heavy body build at age thirty. And then, when you consider that diet is a contributing factor in 35 percent of all cancers, you may find it was something you were eating twenty years ago that was the big risk. No wonder the alcohol — breast cancer link has been hard either to pin down or discount completely.

As a result, doctors are extremely cautious with their advice. "It is quite possible," Sir Richard Doll told me, "that alcohol affects the metabolism of estrogen. So it's possible alcohol could affect the risk of breast cancer by modifying the circulation of the female sex hormones. But the question hasn't been settled yet," he added. "It's not clear yet whether that could be the result of confounding [mixing up] with other aspects of the diet. So I think one can only say that the balance of benefit would be a much smaller amount of alcohol for women than for men." By that, he said, about a drink or a drink and a half per day for women.

Two American researchers, Dr. Arthur Schatzkin and Dr. Matthew Longnecker, pointed out that breast cancer, which claimed forty-six thousand lives in the United States in 1993 (and, in Canada, a predicted 5,600 for 1995), is on the increase. That may be partly accounted for by the fact that as more women are having mammograms, more cases are being detected. They found, after reviewing all the studies, a very small increased risk for women consuming two drinks a day. They concluded that "a causal relationship between alcohol and breast cancer has not been proven. However, the weight of epidemiologic and other types of evidence suggests that something is going on." If there was a risk, they added, alcohol, unlike many other risk factors, was something you could choose to avoid.

Dr. Moira Plant, of the Alcohol Research Group at Edinburgh University, feels that with the number of studies that have failed to find a link, it is unlikely that a connection will now be found. "It doesn't really appear," she said when I spoke to her recently, "that alcohol, certainly in the amount that most women are drinking, has any effect on breast cancer at all."

What should a woman do? Alcohol Concern, the British government-funded addiction agency, in its booklet "A Woman's Guide to Alcohol," sensibly outlines the evidence and points out that other risks actually loom much larger for breast cancer. While no definite link has been established, the organization advises that women, and presumably women who drink, examine their breasts regularly and be alert for changes or lumps.

An authoritative review by British and Dutch scientists in 1993 concluded, as most other studies have, that "there is possibly a weak association between alcohol consumption and breast cancer." But it also concluded: "Any recommendation that women should limit their alcohol consumption specifically in order to reduce their risk of breast cancer cannot be supported or justified by the existing epidemiological evidence."

WOMEN AND ALCOHOL: STILLING FEARS

For the woman who enjoys a drink, it's been a rough decade. It almost seems as if researchers have been lining up to heap on the guilt and anxiety. In Canada and the United States, women have been told they may be harming their babies if they drink even moderately during pregnancy. And women who are breast-feeding and who take a glass of wine risk raised eyebrows. In Europe as well, younger women who drink even occasionally have fingers wagged at them and are warned that they are exposing themselves to a risk of breast cancer — even though, as we saw in the section on cancer, there seems to be very little, if any, risk involved.

It's guilt heaped on guilt. American doctors report that some women are so fearful that their babies may be born deformed, even after modest drinking, that they request abortions. And some doctors, influenced perhaps in spite of themselves by the panic atmosphere, are telling their female patients, pregnant or not: "Why drink at all! It won't do you any good, and it could do you harm."

Possible harm, of course, needs to be carefully considered. Informed decisions need to be made. The possible good women derive from light drinking also deserves attention. It starts, as do so many other issues involving women, with females being free and equal, entitled to enjoy the good things in life — providing they are reasonably safe — without facing reproving looks and public rebukes from people with their own political agendas.

Beyond that, there is the health issue. The main theme of this book has been that moderate alcohol consumption, of wine in particular, offers significant protection against coronary heart disease — the single biggest killer of men and women. That protection kicks in at different life stages for men and women. Atherosclerosis, as we have seen, begins to take a serious hold on men's arteries from the age of thirty on, reaching its peak in the early fifties. Women, protected in their earlier years by estrogen, do not experience heart attacks in large numbers until they reach menopause.

Doctors traditionally have not worried overly about pre-menopausal women having heart attacks. Which is one big reason why the younger woman with heart disease or a heart attack tends to be overlooked in diagnosis and, as studies have shown, does not receive the same level of care as men with similar problems. Obviously men are at greater risk in their thirties and forties. But could it be that women are again receiving second-best advice when they are told they don't need that protection until menopause?

One of the big medical stories of our times is how women, now that they are part of what was formerly the man's world of work, are coming down with men's diseases. Everywhere, as women smoke more, lung cancer is taking over from breast cancer as the leading cause of cancer death among women. Surprisingly, heart attacks, not lung cancer, represent the biggest risk for smokers. Heart disease has been linked directly to smoking. The risks are mitigated somewhat by moderate alcohol intake.

Dr. Linda Bisson, a University of California, Davis, biochemist, puts forward her own reason why it may not be a good idea for women to wait until menopause before starting to drink:

> One of the dangers is suddenly shifting one of the
> energy sources in your body [replacing or augmenting
> some of your usual calories with alcohol calories]. If
> there's not an alcohol problem in your family, and you
> are not at risk of becoming an alcoholic, then occa-
> sional drinking when you're young is a good way of
> keeping your body informed that there is this other
> energy source so that it doesn't shut down the systems
> when if you start drinking later in life.

Her advice to women: "Trust your instincts."

It's difficult advice to take when women are being bombarded with scare stories about deformed babies and breast cancer. It comes down to relative risk. But first you need to know what the risks are.

FETAL ALCOHOL SYNDROME: CREATING A PANIC

Stepping outside for a moment, I could hear the roar of the Pacific rollers thundering on the beach a couple of miles away. Back inside by the stove, Alexa, who is seven, came and sat close. And as the rain cascaded on the roof, bringing down twigs from the redwood trees, she read me some of her favourite poems by Shel Silverstein, including the one about the babysitter who thought her job was to sit on the baby. Alexa is bright, affectionate, chock-full of laughter, and we have continued to write to each other since I stayed the night with her parents at Aptos, south of San Francisco. But if you believe some American health activists, Alexa might well have been born deformed or mentally impaired — because her mother, Sandie, drank modest amounts of wine while she was pregnant with Alexa.

Canada and the United States have, in the last decade, been swept by a panic — a totally irrational wave of fear — over fetal alcohol syndrome (FAS). Women's apprehensions have been stirred up by a deliberate campaign of misinformation to make them believe that even moderate drinking will cause irreparable harm to their babies. Since 1990, every bottle of wine, beer, or spirits sold in the United States has carried this warning: "According to the Surgeon General, women should not drink alcoholic beverages during pregnancy because of the risk of birth defects." In one incident, a pregnant woman was refused service in a restaurant in Tukwila, Washington, in March 1991, and the waiter ostentatiously peeled a label off a bottle of beer, placed it in front of her, and said, "This is just in case you didn't know."

Well-known television personalities have made emotional appeals to women not to touch a drop during pregnancy, and in some Canadian cities, including Toronto, ominous warnings about the consequences of drinking during pregnancy are by law posted in the women's toilets in restaurants and bars, and in beer stores.

There is nothing imaginary or fanciful about FAS. It exists, and it is very serious. The conjunction of drinking and pregnancy, in fact, seems to have aroused basic fears going back to Biblical times and before. Young couples in ancient Carthage and Sparta were forbidden the use of alcohol in case they conceived while intoxicated. In the Bible, an angel warns Samson's mother: "Thou shalt conceive and bear a son. Now therefore beware I pray thee and drink not wine and strong spirit."

In 1834, a select committee of the British House of Commons observed, "Infants born to alcoholic mothers sometimes have a starved, shrivelled and imperfect look." Fetal alcohol syndrome got its name and its modern notoriety first from a French study and then from a study published in 1973 by a group of Washington State researchers who identified the symptoms, including growth and developmental deficiencies, in eight children born to alcoholic mothers.

The public, however, only really became alarmed following the 1979 publication of a searingly emotional book, *Broken Cord* (New York: Harper & Row) in which Michael Dorris described the daunting behavioural problems he encountered raising his adopted FAS child. The panic got another push when two very prominent scientists got their sums wrong. Dr. Ernest Abel and Dr. Robert Sokol of the Fetal Alcohol Research Center in Detroit announced in 1987 that, by their estimates, 1.9 children in every 1,000 were afflicted with FAS. By 1991 the two men had to issue a revised estimate: 0.33 per 1,000 children — only a sixth of their original guess.

No matter how small the chances, any woman who is pregnant is going to worry. And there was plenty to get them worried. Posters and pictures were displayed everywhere showing infants with the terrifying FAS symptoms — small, widespread mongoloid eyes, upturned nose, narrow forehead, long, smooth upper lip, and deformed hands. The captions speak of low birth weight and mental deficiencies. Where symptoms are milder and harder to attribute, they have been given the grab-bag name, fetal alcohol effect (FAE). It's a daring woman these days in Regina, Saskatchewan, or Waco, Texas, who, while visibly pregnant, accepts a drink at a party; even women who smoke while pregnant — a much more threatening activity than light drinking — are more tolerated.

So where is the evidence for this scourge sweeping the maternity units of America? "FAS does exist," says Dr. Moira Plant, who wrote a book on the subject in 1985: *Women, Drinking, and Pregnancy* (London: Tavistock Publications) and who is now at work on a book on women and alcohol. "There's no question about that." But, she says, women who are light drinkers have nothing to fear; FAS children are born only to mothers who could be categorized as alcoholics and who, in addition, are usually suffering from severe deprivation.

And what are the facts on FAS?

Fact: Nearly all FAS children are born to inner city African-American women or to Native women living either in city slums or on reservations. Says Dr. Abel: "If you look at cities that are characterized by minorities, you're looking at 2 [FAS infants] per 1,000, which is very high. If you look at Denver or Seattle [cities generally free of downtown black ghettos], you find there are almost no cases."

Fact: Even amongst these women drinking heavily and living in the most appalling circumstances, only about 30 percent of their babies are born FAS.

Fact: FAS is almost unknown among the middle classes —
the very people likely to read the warnings on bottles and to
become alarmed by the scare campaign. A 1987 study of 32,870
California mothers, 47 percent of whom drank alcohol during
pregnancy, uncovered not a single case of a child with the classic FAS symptoms.

Most women anyway, says Dr. Plant, tend to drink very
little during pregnancy. They just don't have the taste for alcohol. But in the United States and Canada, which is feeling the
border slopover of the American panic, drinking levels among
pregnant women have sunk close to zero. Dr. Plant suspects
FAS is more than simply a question of heavy drinking. "Women
generally tend to have a poorer nutritional status than men," she
told me. "Often what we think of as alcohol problems are really nutritional problems. Social deprivation to me is one of the
major health issues. It's unfair to say it's what these women are
drinking. It's what's happened to them. They are isolated, lonely, and not 100 percent responsible for where they are."

The most conclusive evidence yet that FAS should not be
a concern for any but a tiny minority of women came from a
study carried out in Dundee, Scotland, and published in the
British Medical Journal in 1991. Instead of focusing on a vulnerable portion of the population, the researchers simply signed
up the first 846 women who walked through the door at local
prenatal care facilities. Thus it included women from a wide
range of economic and social strata.

The women's drinking habits were carefully noted, and 592
of the children born later were monitored until they reached
the age of eighteen months. The researchers decided that it was
only after the mothers had consumed alcohol at a rate of twelve
drinks a week or more that the children showed any reduction
in motor or mental development. And they concluded that, as
there was no detectable damage at moderate rates of drinking,

there was no reason why women should not drink moderately while pregnant.

A sensible limit, they suggested, would be eight British units a week or about one drink a day. Alcohol Concern, the British addiction agency, takes a low-key approach to FAS. In its booklet "A Woman's Guide to Alcohol," it says that most research shows FAS babies are born to women drinking the weekly equivalent of two bottles of spirits or eight bottles of wine. "Many women who have FAS babies also have poor diets or experience poor social conditions," it notes.

What does Alcohol Concern consider a safe drinking limit for women who are pregnant? While the American Surgeon General has advised no drinking at all, it notes, "there now seems to be general agreement amongst European doctors that a [British] unit of alcohol a day has a very low risk level." In North America, too, there are those who take issue with the Surgeon General's advice. Genevieve Knupfer, of the Alcohol Research Group at Berkeley, California, wrote in the *British Journal of Addiction* in 1991, "There is no evidence that light drinking by pregnant women harms the fetus." She defined light drinking as two drinks about four to six times a week.

Dr. Gideon Koren, a professor of pediatrics and pharmacology at the University of Toronto, notes that more than half of all pregnancies are unplanned, and most adult women drink socially. The result is that thousands of women drink before they know they are pregnant. Those dire warnings about FAS, says Professor Koren, induce a "level of anxiety in these women [that] is excessive, and their readiness to terminate an otherwise wanted pregnancy is high." No amount of sensible advice, though, now seems enough to shake the conviction many North American women hold — that even the smallest amount of alcohol while they are pregnant will have horrible consequences. A recent survey showed that ill-informed community workers are still telling women that even a single drink will harm their unborn babies.

What was the reason for the North American panic? I asked Alexa's father, who happens to be Dr. Wells Shoemaker, a pediatrician who owns a small winery, and who, not unnaturally, has given a good deal of thought to the issue.

"It's really a triumph of politics," he explained. The neo-prohibitionists, he said, were looking for an issue to attack drinking generally. In the wake of the great North American battle over abortion, "the fetus was an important topic." Tying drinking and harm to the fetus together, he said, "became a useful 'gotcha!' It had a lot of emotional appeal."

The fact that FAS and FAE had hardly any application at all for most women was conveniently overlooked or concealed. The real tragedy of FAS is missed. Its existence in North America, and its almost total absence from Europe — even in the Mediterranean countries where alcohol consumption is high in wine terms — is no mystery. It is partly a consequence of the criminal lack of proper prenatal care provided for poor mothers in the United States. And in both Canada and the United States, the high incidence of FAS among Native children speaks volumes for the sorry condition of the Aboriginal people. As for FAE, it has come in for criticism as being just a vague collection of symptoms with no easily explained cause. Says Dr. Plant: "It seems to have been made into a sort of garbage can into which everyone can throw any symptoms that puzzle them."

Asked for her view on a reasonable drinking limit for pregnant women, Dr. Plant said:

The last multi-centre study showed that up to ten
units a week [about a drink a day] has not shown any
measurable effect on the child. There has been some

evidence that at levels slightly higher than that there's been a decreased birth weight, but the child catches up so quickly that it could not be rated as an alcohol-related thing. I would stick at one or two drinks once or twice a week. There hasn't been any evidence that at those levels there's any noticeable effect.

Should a woman drink if she's breast-feeding her child? "Alcohol does pass through to the baby," said Dr. Plant. "Most mothers who drink recognize that. The baby may sleep well after its ten o'clock feed if the mother has had a couple of drinks. But so far as I am aware, there is no evidence to suggest it passes through in quantities that would actually damage the baby."

She discounted any possibility that women who are heavy drinkers would harm their babies through breast-feeding. "A woman with a drinking problem would probably not be breast-feeding," she said. "You need to be organized, very much in control of the situation to breast-feed."

Should women drink less than men? In spite of the recent Danish study suggesting that women who drink the same amount as men get the same amount of protection against all-cause mortality as men do, Dr. Plant believes that for now it's better to be conservative. "I think women do have to drink less than men because of their smaller size. Also women have more difficulty breaking down the alcohol compared with men because men have an extra enzyme in their stomachs that allows them to absorb alcohol faster." The trouble is, said the Edinburgh researcher, that nearly all the research on drinking up to now has been done on men. Even the questions asked in surveys — like, "Have you ever gone to work with a hangover?" — apply more to men than, say, a mother at home.

That's about to change, she says. Thanks to the presence of a whole new generation of women researchers in the alcohol field, "we will be finding out an enormous amount in the next five or six years about women and alcohol. And I suspect some of it will be very different from what we think we know at the minute."

Aging Well

At one time it was considered enough just to live a long time. Advanced age brought love, respect, and a seat in the corner by the fire. The elderly were essentially static figures surrounded by the loving care of the family. Now we know it's different. Sons and daughters are too busy to care for Mom or Dad when they're getting on, and the spectre of the nursing home induces feelings of unease, even of panic, as the years tumble by.

If you reach sixty-five these days, you can expect to live another seventeen years. They can be the worst years — or the best years. We know now the trick is not to reach a grand old age, but to reach it in cracking shape. We know we have to make those extra years count. So attitudes towards aging have changed. Gone the age of old people sitting in the corner. Welcome instead the age of the octogenarian athlete. At the pool where I swim every day a woman of eighty-three recently received an award for swimming fourteen hundred kilometres — at about a kilometre a day!

The elderly are to be found not just gardening or lawn bowling (although both are wonderful activities), but on the tennis courts, in the gym, on mountain tops, and even taking part in marathons. They are careful of their weight, their blood pressure, and their diet. And, recognizing that it is the brain above all things that needs exercise, they attend night school or college and travel the world, taking over many universities in summer under the auspices of the Elderhostel programs.

The formula for a healthful, vigorous old age is sought like the holy grail, not only by the aging, but also by scientists in the blossoming field of geriatrics. One of the best studies to identify the factors that contribute to a healthy, active old age was conducted in Alameda County, California, and published in the *American Journal of Public Health* in 1989. Dr. Jack M. Guralnik of the National Institute on Aging and George A. Kaplan of the California Department of Health Services in 1965 questioned 841 people born before 1920 about their health and activity patterns. Nineteen years later they checked on the survivors of this group — which had now been whittled down to 496 by death. The subjects, by then aged between sixty-five and eighty-nine, were asked about everyday activities like shopping, gardening, climbing stairs, and walking half a mile. But they were also questioned about rigorous physical activities like jogging, cycling, tennis, dancing, and walking for exercise.

About a quarter — 107 individuals — were zippy oldsters who were counted as "high-functioning." On the down side, being a smoker, having high blood pressure, being poor, or being black were factors contributing to an early death or disability. And among the factors that kept the spark alive in those high-functioners: keeping to a moderate weight, eating breakfast regularly, and consuming moderate amounts of alcohol.

"Those with moderate alcohol intake were 2.4 times more likely to have high function at follow-up than abstainers and 1.7 times more likely to have high function than heavy drinkers," the team reported. The results should have surprised no one. A number of studies have supported the idea that a glass of wine or beer contribute to quality of life for the elderly. It helps to explain why, even in the United States, where an unusually high proportion of the population are abstainers, wine is served in more than half the hospitals, and the "cocktail hour" is now part of the routine in most nursing homes.

Dr. Robert Stepto, a member of the Chicago Board of Health, spoke of the use of wine in hospitals: "I believe we should intensively promote the therapeutic uses of wine. This would involve education of hospital personnel, physicians, and patients."

Robert Kastenbaum, a professor of psychology at Wayne State University, puts it this way: "Wine is a food and a drug. But it is also a symbol of adult mutual gratification. There is a world of difference between ordering an old man to take his medicine, and inviting him to have a drink. The former action confirms his opinion that he is an impaired organism to be processed and serviced by impersonal means. The latter action suggests that he is still regarded as a grown-up, one who is capable of giving and receiving adult gratifications."

And that little drop of wine or beer or glass of spirits seems to help: researchers at Indiana State and Duke universities have kept track for more than twenty years of nearly four thousand twins who were Second World War veterans, keeping a careful tally on their drinking habits. The latest check on the cognitive skills of these men, now mostly in their sixties, seventies, or eighties, shows those who have one or two drinks a day score higher than their brothers who either abstain or drink more or less than that amount.

A second study of six thousand Americans over sixty-five confirmed that moderate drinkers performed better in tests of their mental ability. Even more surprising were the results of a study of bone mineral density in the elderly published in the *British Medical Journal* in 1993. Osteoporosis, the weakening of the bones, is a major cause of disability as we get older, particularly for women. That's one reason — to strengthen the bones — that millions of women past menopause now take estrogen supplements. Researchers from the University of California, San Diego, measured the bone mineral density of a group of 182 men and 267 women in the early 1970s when they were all over the age of forty-five, also making a note of their drinking habits. Sixteen to nineteen years later the same people were checked again.

An interesting pattern emerged. Even after allowing for smoking and, in the women, estrogen replacement therapy, the "social" or moderate drinkers showed higher bone density levels — a powerful indicator of a healthy old age.

This is not to suggest that drinking is the panacea for aging and that everyone over sixty-five should take it up. Dr. Curtis Ellison, the Boston cardiologist who has spoken out frequently on the health benefits of drinking, says there is a small minority of the elderly for whom it could be a peril. "We know that there are a number of people who start to abuse alcohol when they become depressed," he says. "Particularly elderly widows who are lonely."

But Dr. Arthur Klatsky talks about the social benefits people in nursing homes especially derive from that glass of wine or beer. "There are studies that show more social interaction, they become more talkative. It's really not surprising: that's why people drink in general."

George Burns would agree. As I write this, the American comedian is ninety-seven and promising everyone he will fulfill his engagement to appear at the London Palladium for his one hundredth birthday. Burns's recipe for longevity, rather on the excessive side, it must be admitted, includes five martinis a day.

THE CASE OF THE MISSING CALORIES

Will drinking wine make you fat? Logic suggests that regular wine consumption — or drinking any alcoholic beverage for that matter — should add to your weight. Alcohol, after all, equals calories. But the opposite may be true, especially for women. The reasons are a real mystery.

As Dr. Andrew Prentice at the Dunn Clinical Nutrition Centre at Cambridge explained it to me, instead of being fatter as a result of their drinking, most people seem to lose weight. The evidence, he said, comes from the American Nurses' Health Study, which recorded the heights, weights, and drinking and eating patterns of ninety thousand women aged thirty to fifty-five. You'd expect that those who took on extra calories through drinking would be fatter. Not so. "The fattest group," said Dr. Prentice, "consisted of the women who didn't drink at all." And up to a rate of several drinks a day, the more these women drank, the less they weighed. "People who drink," said Dr. Prentice, just to make sure I understood this odd proposition, "tend to be slimmer."

The same held true for men followed in the Health Professionals' Follow-Up Study, although they did not show as dramatic a slimming effect from the alcohol as the women did. So where were the calories going? When the Cambridge team looked at the nurses' total intake, they didn't appear to be cutting back on their food to compensate for their drinking. "If you buy the argument that the alcohol calories are additive," said the doctor, "and that people are slimmer in spite of having a considerably higher energy intake, then you have to say either that those people are much more physically active — which is not likely — or there is something very peculiar about alcohol calories."

Were the calories in the drinks "empty calories," or were they somehow being wasted? The Cambridge team set out to find out. They selected five healthy males in their thirties (you wonder why they didn't use women, where the effect is more pronounced) and placed them in a calorimeter for thirty-six hours. A calorimeter is a sealed unit in which all intakes are measured so that researchers can accurately gauge energy consumption and expenditure. The five subjects ate normal food the first day and food with alcohol the second day, and the rate at which they burned calories was closely monitored. And at the end the mystery was still unsolved. The men had burned up the alcohol calories first, but did not store fat. Confirming this finding, Dr. Prentice says a colleague at Oxford has placed tiny catheters inside the stomachs of volunteers to observe the actual fat-building process. But when alcohol is administered, no fat is stored.

What about beer bellies — where elbow hoisting obviously does lead to excessive avoirdupois? "That's a different situation," said the doctor. "You have a lot of carbohydrates coming on board with the alcohol. And I think it's a case of substitution — they're drinking a lot of beer instead of eating."

The question of the missing calories is creating intense interest since it relates to obesity, the prevalence of which is of increasing worry to doctors in North America and Europe. (The incidence of obesity has doubled in Britain in the last decade alone, and in North America, one-third of adults are overweight.) According to a soon-to-be published National Institute of Health study from Beltsville, Maryland, among people on a high-fat diet, moderate drinkers were better able to control their weight than abstainers. Another new U.S. study shows that women who are light drinkers weigh on average two to three kilograms less than abstainers, although the effect was not as pronounced with men.

Dr. Prentice suspects that alcohol may act to suppress the appetite — if not at the time it is consumed, then the following day. But American researchers theorize that alcohol revs up the metabolic process, causing the body to burn calories more effectively. It's all new frontier science, as the researchers look for those missing calories. Sounds like a case for Sherlock Holmes.

WINE FOR BRAIN POWER?

Does drinking wine make you rich and smart? It depends how you read the figures. In 1990 two researchers at Washington University in St. Louis, Hugh Klein and David J. Pittman, posed the question: what distinguishes people who drink either beer, wine, or spirits? After surveying the literature and polling more than one thousand drinkers, they published their results in the *Journal of Substance Abuse*.

Wine, they found, was the only drink directly related to educational attainment. In other words, the higher your educational qualifications, the more likely you were to be a wine drinker. Wine preference also went up with income. Women were more likely to be wine drinkers, and there was a tendency for people to switch to wine from beer and spirits as they got older. Wine drinkers were also found to be more moderate in their intakes, and in 75 percent of cases, the wine was consumed at home. Eighty-two percent of the time, the wine went with a meal, usually dinner.

These results make it easy to understand U.S. Bureau of Statistics reports on drinking and driving arrests, which show 54 percent of the drivers had been consuming beer, 23 percent spirits, 2 percent wine, and the remainder a mixture of drinks. So does drinking wine make you richer, smarter, and a safer driver to boot? I wouldn't bet on it.

For Flatulence: One Half-Bottle of Alsace

Dr. Emmerick Maury, a French general practitioner who believed fervently in the healthful qualities of wine, left nothing to chance when he wrote a bestseller, which in 1974 was translated into English as *Wine Is the Best Medicine*. Dr. Maury, also an acupuncture specialist and homeopath, taught that wine was part of a healthful diet, and was also an invaluable remedy to supplement more conventional medical treatments.

Not content with simply recommending wine as a general tonic, the doctor was quite precise about which wines should be taken for specific conditions. Although most of his recommendations would raise a smile from knowledgeable scientists, a few have proved to have some validity in light of the newest research. For osteoporosis, the loss of calcium in the bones, for example, his recipe was to drink two glasses of Burgundy with the meal one day and two glasses of Bordeaux the next. Recent studies, while not related to wine specifically, have shown that moderate alcohol consumption helps stave off osteoporosis. The following are some of Dr. Maury's prescriptions.

Nervous depression: One or two glasses of Médoc before and during meals.

Flatulence: Half a bottle per day of dry, young, white Alsace wine, divided between lunch and dinner.

Fever: One bottle of dry or brut Champagne per day, taken in doses of one glass every hour.

Diarrhea: One glass of young Beaujolais before and after meals.

Allergies: Médoc, two glasses per meal.

Constipation: White wines from Anjou or Vouvray.

Cystitis (inflammation of the bladder): One or two glasses per meal of sweet or semi-sweet white wines from Anjou.

Gallstones: Dry, white wines, low in alcohol, from the Sancerre or Pouilly region.

Gout: Again, light white wines from Sancerre or Pouilly, or rose wines from Provence.

Influenza: Wines from Côtes du Rhône, half a bottle a day taken, during the feverish stage, in three or four equal portions, heated in a double-boiler at 140 degrees Fahrenheit with 1 tablespoon of cinnamon, 5 teaspoons of sugar, and some lemon peel.

Menopause: Two glasses per meal of Bordeaux wine from the Médoc region.

Obesity: One bottle per day of Rosé wine from Provence or dry, white wine from Sancerre, both low in sugar and alcohol.

Old age: Red wines from the Aloxe-Corton region or light, dry wines such as the non-carbonated Champagne wines.

Rheumatism: Dry, light wines, such as the non-carbonated wines of Champagne, two glasses per meal.

Pregnancy: Dr. Maury's recommendation of two glasses of light, red, 10 percent alcohol Burgundy with each meal would raise the eyebrows of some modern gynecologists, although Dr. Maury is in line with the newest science when he mentions the antioxidant function these wines perform in removing toxins.

Stomach or hiatus hernia: Two glasses per meal of medium-dry champagne.

Dr. Maury's homeopathic background preaches that, with most things, a little can help, a lot can hurt. Drawing on this, Dr. Maury writes, "Everything is a question of moderation, the use of wine like everything else."

CHAPTER VII

Deciding for Yourself

THE DOCTOR'S DILEMMA

Professor Michael Marmot was on the spot. I had picked him up at Toronto's Pearson International Airport and was driving him to his hotel. It was a mild December evening, and the city spread out, a brilliant carpet of lights, beside the Queen Elizabeth Way. But the professor was having a problem. Not with my driving, I hope, but over the question I had just asked him.

Marmot, professor of epidemiology and public health at University College in London, has a significant influence over what people in Britain — and elsewhere too — eat and drink. When I spoke to him he was under fire from the British biscuit and cake industry. As chairman of the Committee on the Medical Aspects of Food Policy (COMA) he had just released a nutrition blueprint that came down hard on the traditional British sweet tooth. (The report, by the way, reviewed the latest evidence on antioxidants and found it "persuasive.")

Less well-known is Professor Marmot's long-standing connection with the alcohol and wine issue, and that's what I wanted to talk to him about. Only he is always on the go. A couple of times I'd tried to see him in London, and found he was in Toronto. When I was in Toronto, he was in Copenhagen. Finally it was decided, my best chance of seeing him was to pick him up at the airport as he scooted downtown for yet another meeting. For a man who is portrayed as a tiger by his opponents, he turned out to be surprisingly mild and modest as he lugged his overnight bag through the arrivals gate. I led him to the car, invited him to get in, thrust a miniature tape recorder into his hand, and more or less asked him to talk.

Does alcohol in moderation protect from coronary heart disease? He had no doubts at all. "I am persuaded by the evidence that moderate alcohol consumption is related to lower coronary risk. I first published on this fourteen or fifteen years ago and I've reviewed the evidence a couple of times since. And it just gets stronger."

Should a moderate intake of alcohol then be part of a healthy diet? This, according to the tape, is what he replied: "Well, my own feeling is ... is that ... " He stumbles, hesitates, then sighs. "Um, in a way you've got to, er ... " Sighs. "In a way, you've got to ... it's up to the scientific research to prove, well, I'm not quite clear whether I believe this or not. But I think it's more important, in a way, to point out the hazards, that [if] people are going to drink alcohol they don't need doctors to prescribe it. People are going to drink alcohol because they enjoy it. It's really more important for medical science to point out its hazards."

I don't for a moment want to poke fun at Professor Marmot. I have a huge respect for him. He had just gotten off a plane after a trans-Atlantic flight and none of us are at our best at such moments. But in that unguarded moment, his reply revealed the dilemma in which many scientists and doctors find themselves when they are asked for their advice on moderate wine or alcohol consumption. They are scared silly of saying publicly that a glass or two a day is good for you in case thousands take it the wrong way and become roaring drunks. Often the very scientists who have come up with the most convincing evidence of alcohol's benefits are at pains to keep their findings a secret from the general public.

You have to have some sympathy for them. Doctors more than anyone see the tragic results of alcoholism: the strokes, the cancers, the cirrhosis, the shattered families, the broken bodies following traffic accidents. They fear, in showing any flexibility on the issue, that they will earn the criticism of alcohol abuse professionals, as well as their colleagues. But, as in war, truth in this campaign is often the first casualty.

The whole debate on drinking and health, in fact, has been marked by a series of forward and backward movements not unlike the tango. If the news about drinking becomes too positive, you can be sure of a headline in tomorrow's paper proclaiming the whole thing a hoax. It almost sounds as if it's being stage-managed. Chapter III looks at the efforts of Professor Hugh Tunstall-Pedoe to downplay the French Paradox, even though the World Health Organization (WHO)'s Monica study, of which he was coordinator, confirmed its existence.

Two weeks after Tunstall-Pedoe expressed his doubts, Hans Emblad, Swedish director of the WHO Program on Substance Abuse, made headlines around the world when he announced, "The less you drink the better." Flying in the face of more than sixty reports confirming the beneficial effects of wine and alcohol drunk in moderation, Emblad said, "We are not actually campaigning for a teetotal world, but I suppose if you take our message to its logical conclusion, the optimal drinking level should be zero."

And the research by leading scientists showing that abstainers are at greater risk of heart disease than moderate drinkers? The studies, said Emblad, were "to a large extent inspired by commercial purposes." In other words, it was a plot by the drinks industry.

The statement could hardly have been more insulting to scientists of great eminence like Britain's Sir Richard Doll, who had only just produced a study of British physicians showing that moderate drinking was protective against coronary heart disease. Or, for that matter, to Professor Marmot who, in 1991, produced yet another study confirming the existence of the U-shaped curve.

The unstoppable Mr. Emblad had another point to make. Even if moderate alcohol was protective, he said, you could achieve the maximum benefit by consuming less than one glass every other day. This, in fact, contradicts the large mass of studies that show maximum benefit occurs at a level of one to three drinks a day, and suggests Emblad hasn't even been listening to WHO's own experts. A study on cardiovascular disease published by the WHO Scientific Group only a short time before said that, for coronary heart disease, "the risk is greater for non-drinkers ... It can be concluded, therefore, that moderate drinking (1–3 drinks per day) provides a moderate protective effect against cardiovascular disease compared with abstention and heavy drinking."

But even the WHO doctors, after declaring that moderate drinking is beneficial, suggested: "It is probably better to conclude that moderate consumption of alcohol does no harm to the cardiovascular system than to emphasize its protective effect because any public health encouragement to consume alcohol would often be misinterpreted and lead to excessive intakes with increased risk for total mortality." In other words, prevaricate, lie. Don't tell the public the truth. They're not to be trusted. Even if the truth saves lives.

WHO can't be faulted for trying to stem alcohol abuse, or for trying to discourage the introduction of alcohol into Third World countries where heart disease rates are low and people are simply not accustomed to alcohol. But its stance towards the developed world, where although there certainly is a minority who abuse alcohol, there is also a long tradition of civilized drinking, gives concern. Instead of simply targeting alcohol abuse there, WHO has adopted a zealous, blinkered approach more in tune with the nineteenth-century temperance movement than with modern tastes and needs.

Its European Alcohol Action Plan released in 1993, for instance, calls for a blanket reduction in alcohol consumption throughout Europe of 25 percent. No talk here of the health benefits of wine and alcohol. No discussion of the cultural significance of wine in many countries. No careful analysis of the larger number of lives saved through moderate alcohol consumption versus the smaller number of lives lost through alcohol abuse. None of that. Simply a blanket policy: Booze is bad.

The attempts to discount the potential health benefits of moderate wine and alcohol consumption continue. As we have seen, Renaud's French Paradox has attracted much criticism. The latest to put the paradox to the test is Dr. Michael Criqui, a prominent cardiologist and epidemiologist at the University of California's San Diego School of Medicine. With colleague Brenda Ringel, he carried out an exhaustive examination of alcohol, diet, and mortality data from twenty-one developed countries, including Britain, the United States, France, New Zealand, and Australia, between 1965 and 1988. And after all that, when the study was published in *The Lancet* in December 1994, he could only confirm what St. Leger, with the slimmest of resources, had discovered fifteen years earlier: that wine is best.

High animal fat consumption, Criqui found, nearly always meant high cardiac rates — except in France and, to a lesser degree, Switzerland. Fresh fruit consumption was a big plus, indicating healthy hearts. Countries with high beer and spirit consumption were only so-so, showing a modest reduction in CHD rates. "The strongest and most consistent correlation," Criqui and Ringel found, was with wine. High wine consumption time and time again equalled low coronary heart disease rates. France, with the highest alcohol and wine consumption of all, they found, consistently had the lowest

CHD rates next to Japan. Measuring deaths from all diseases, France went from eighth lowest position in 1980 to sixth place in 1988.

It sounds like good news. But Criqui wasn't finished. After examining overall mortality figures he announced that, although wine was lifesaving, it didn't seem to help overall mortality (a finding clearly contradicted by the Danish study). The good that wine did now in preventing heart disease, he seemed to be suggesting, was wiped out down the road because too many people overindulged and died of cancer or cirrhosis or some other dreadful disease linked to alcoholism.

The finding puzzled some of Criqui's friends and colleagues. Dr. Curtis Ellison, a cardiologist at the University of Boston medical school, believes Criqui was quite right in finding that wine provided the greatest benefit. "Then he carried it a little too far and made what I thought were extremely inappropriate statements. He said total mortality [in wine-drinking countries] is no lower. As a matter of fact it is lower." Even if people in wine-drinking countries live only 2.5 years or so longer, it still means an enormous difference for many people, said Ellison. "It could mean one person in every four is living ten years longer." What wouldn't most of us give for another ten years! "A small increase [in longevity] can be very striking," he said.

Criqui is basing his warning on a theory that, according to the Boston doctor, has been discredited, but that is still used constantly by addiction professionals. The theory is that as the average alcohol consumption in a country increases, so does the amount of alcohol-caused illness and death. "It doesn't make sense," said Ellison. "It ain't so."

It might, of course, be true for countries like Finland with a reputation for alcohol abuse and binge drinking. But to suggest that because Cindy Moderate, a careful modern young woman in Toronto, decides to have a glass of wine with her dinner, there will be a chain reaction and some poor addicted wretch at the other end of the alcohol consumption ladder will die a miserable death, does, as Ellison suggests, beggar belief. "Several people," said Ellison, tactfully dismissing Criqui's warning, "said he should have known better."

John Duffy, a statistician with Edinburgh University's Alcohol Research Group, has been equally outspoken about the "average drinking level" theory. "It's absolute madness," he says. "It would be a strange world if a population with a high proportion of heavy drinkers didn't have a high average level of consumption. But discouraging moderate drinkers from drinking, while it might bring the average down, doesn't solve the problem. If you want to reduce the population of heavy drinkers," says Duffy, "you have to persuade heavy drinkers to drink less."

Neither Criqui's argument nor Ellison and Duffy's rebuttals will, of course, put the matter to rest. New objections to the wine and health argument pop up all the time. With more studies being publicized, you are freer to decide for yourself. That's if you don't have a problem with alcohol. But what happens if you do?

Too Much of a Good Thing

 Ask the guy at the beer store buying his two-four for the Saturday night blast what the biggest hazard is for heavy drinkers. He'll look a bit puzzled, then hazard, "Cirrhosis?" That's what he's heard anyway. Ask his wife and you'll get a different answer. Ask a police officer and you'll get a third answer.

Cirrhosis of the liver — the gradual death of the liver as it becomes progressively scarred — is a comparatively rare disease in North America. Rates in France are twice as high, although the figures are deceptive. The high rates are found in the north of France, where beer and spirits are commonly consumed, while the rate in the wine-drinking southwest is lower than that in the United States. To put it in perspective, in Canada in 1990, 762 people died of alcoholic cirrhosis. In the same year one hundred times as many people — seventy-seven thousand — died of cardiovascular diseases. The same ratio holds true in the United States.

Cirrhosis, half the cases of which are caused by heavy drinking, is a miserable disease leading in the majority of cases to a most unpleasant death. The more you drink, the more likely you are to get it, until, at a level of six drinks a day or more, you are eighteen times more likely to get it than an abstainer. And yet, in a broader sense, cirrhosis is not by any means the worst consequence of alcohol abuse. The difference between smokers and heavy drinkers, it used to be said, was that drinkers hurt others while smokers hurt only themselves. Today we know about the effects of secondhand smoke and the saying, as far as cigarettes are concerned, is no longer true. But it's as accurate as ever when it comes to drinking.

Addiction agencies, which try to quantify these things, have a hard time putting a figure on the damage that excessive drinking causes. How do you measure the lives of innocent people killed by drunken drivers? How do you measure the hurt of a child, quoted by Margaret Cork in her book, *Forgotten Children* (Toronto: Alcoholism and Drug Addiction, 1969), who said, "Dad's spoiled every Christmas I can remember because he smashed the tree." Or worse, the hurt of children who live daily with the sound of screams and thumps from their parents' bedrooms. How do you measure a woman's bruises and broken bones? How do you put a price on random violence, child abuse, suicide, and murder?

A decade ago it was estimated that alcohol abuse cost Canada nearly $12 billion and contributed to one death in ten. In 1993, the U.S. Assistant Secretary for Health, Dr. Philip Lee, estimated that alcohol contributed to one hundred thousand deaths a year and cost $86 billion. Such figures are necessarily arbitrary, and the news isn't all bad. In most developed countries, including Canada and the United States, the number of deaths caused by drunk drivers has decreased dramatically in the last decade. Apart from a hardcore group of incorrigibles — and young drivers who have yet to learn — it's now not the done thing to drive home one over the eight.

It's legitimate to ask, though, whether people interested enough in their health to read this book are likely to end up in the statistical tables dealing with alcohol-linked deaths or accidents. The latest British Department of Transport figures show, for example, that the peak age for drinking-and-driving fatalities is twenty, with nearly 60 percent of these accidents being caused by people seventeen to thirty. There are no exact figures for North America, but the peak age is between sixteen and thirty-five. The age of concern for people who want to protect themselves from coronary heart disease usually starts, in men, at thirty and, in women, at menopause. Men in their teens and twenties who drink to excess are not, normally, doing it for their health.

If excessive alcohol consumption exacts high social costs, it's also true that it results in a good deal of disease and death. The risk profile for alcohol consumption is, after all, a U-shaped one. Moderate drinkers fare better, not just in terms of coronary heart disease, but in all disease mortality, than do abstainers. But the curve soon starts to sweep upwards, indicating that, once you go from moderate into heavy drinking, there is a price to be paid.

"If you were only worried about your heart," Robin Room, vice president of research for the Addiction Research Foundation in Toronto, told me, "then you could drink a great deal. But there's more to our bodies than our hearts."

The figures bear him out. An American Cancer Society study of more than a quarter of a million men aged forty to fifty-nine, for example, showed that even those drinking six or more drinks a day were still less likely to die of coronary heart disease than abstainers (although the maximum protection occurred at a level of two drinks a day). But the big boozers probably wouldn't live to gloat over their abstaining neighbours: the study finds those who imbibe six or more drinks a day are 60 percent more likely to die of some form of cancer; 150 percent more likely to commit suicide; 73 percent more likely to die in an accident; and six times as likely to get cancer of the oral cavity or the esophagus.

The risks for heavy drinkers don't end there. Hypertension — high blood pressure — is a consistent risk factor for coronary disease. A University of Birmingham study attributed 10 to 20 percent of hypertension in that British city to heavy alcohol consumption. After looking at sixty population studies,

Dr. Arthur Klatsky, the Oakland, California, cardiologist who was one of the first to identify the protective benefits of alcohol, says blood pressure levels start to go up with three drinks or more a day.

Professor Michael Marmot at University College, London, and an international team of scientists confirmed in a 1994 INTERSALT study that blood pressure started to go up with three or four or more drinks a day. Marmot has spoken of the "narrow window of opportunity," by which he means that, while significant CHD protection occurs at a level of one or two drinks a day, go much beyond that and the benefits may soon be outstripped by the dangers. It sounds discouraging, even dangerous, to consider drinking for the sake of your health. But read on — knowing your limit and risk is half the battle.

SETTING SENSIBLE LIMITS

In 1862, British neurologist Sir Francis Anstie, with nothing more to go on than general observations of his patients, proposed a daily alcohol guide for the general public of about 35 grams or 45 millilitres of pure ethyl alcohol a day — equivalent to about half a litre of wine or a litre of beer. The Anstie rule was all the medical profession had to go on for more than one hundred years. Now everyone's getting into the act. Setting sensible limits for alcohol consumption has become a cottage industry in the addiction field. And you know what — Anstie wasn't far off the mark in the first place.

Some would say his "limit" was a little on the generous side. But most studies show no harm — and a good deal of benefit — accruing to those who consume up to three drinks a day. To be on the safe side, most experts, including those at Canada's Addiction Research Foundation (ARF), set the figure at two, usually with a lower figure for women. In Australia the advised limit for men is three drinks a day — just about where Anstie put it — and for women, half that.

Britain, of course, had to be different. Several years ago a government body, the Health Education Authority, came out with its "Sensible Drinking Advice." At a consumption rate of twenty-one units per week for men and fourteen for women, drinkers, it said, were not likely to come to harm.

Where the British have come unstuck is basing their unit, consisting of 8 grams or 10 millilitres of alcohol, on the miserly drinks (apart from beer) poured in British pubs. It equals half a pint of beer, a small glass of wine, or a minuscule serving of spirits.

But the British — like Canadians and Americans — are increasingly doing their drinking at home. And when people do their own pouring, they don't stick to those tiny pub portions. When the consumer magazine *Which* measured the number of British units in typical drinks, it also found alarming discrepancies. A small glass of Australian Jacob's Creek red wine — one of the most popular brands — equalled 1.6 units and a 275 millilitre bottle of Carlsberg lager came in at 2.5 units. Most alarming of all — a 440 millilitre can of Tennent's Super lager tipped the scale at 4 units. No wonder that according to a survey, two-thirds of the British public really have no idea what a unit amounts to.

Canada and the United States operate in the real world. ARF in Toronto, in line with other agencies on this continent, defines a drink as 13.6 grams of alcohol, equivalent to a regular 12 ounce or 341 millilitre bottle of beer (5 percent alcohol by volume), a 5 ounce or 142 millilitre glass of table wine

(12 percent alcohol) or a 1.5 ounce or 43 millilitre serving of spirits (40 percent alcohol). That's a little more than 50 percent larger than the shrimpy and deceptive British unit.

The British "sensible advice" is under review as I write this. And none too soon. That weekly total approach could actually encourage binge drinking — the most dangerous form of consumption. Hearing that twenty-one units a week — about fourteen North American drinks — is safe, it's easy for British drinkers to fool themselves that, by taking all fourteen drinks on the weekend, they'll come to no harm. That's not what the experts are saying.

"What we need," said Professor Martin Plant when I called on him in Edinburgh, "is a message that emphasizes the *pattern* of drinking." (North American addiction experts have spoken of a similar need.) Plant, of the Alcohol Research Group at Edinburgh University and husband of Moira Plant, was really the first person in the addiction field to rip away much of the hypocrisy surrounding drinking limits. In a speech in Toronto in 1994 that got big headlines on both sides of the Atlantic he declared, "The alcohol field is highly politicized, and some of the interlocuters have been motivated by ideology and emotion rather than by the force of the evidence itself." We had, he suggested, been fixated on the evils of alcohol, when "study after study supported the view that drinking does have tangible health benefits. Moreover, most drinkers appear to consume at levels consistent with these benefits. This fact seems to make some people uncomfortable."

He confronted head-on the argument put forward by many people in the addiction field that, by reducing the *average* level of drinking in a country, you reduce the amount of drinking problems. It was an appealing notion: "If we all drank a bit less we would all be better off." But, said Plant, it amounted to dealing with one person's fever by telling other people to take a cold shower. And the force of the argument was considerably weakened where health benefits are associated with moderate drinking. At present, he said, there was little attempt to acknowledge the importance of this positive evidence or integrate it into advice on drinking. "This failure is curious and clearly warrants rectification."

There was little to be afraid of: "Surveys of alcohol consumption in Britain indicate that only a small minority [less than 2 percent of women and 10 to 12 percent of men, similar to Canadian figures] consume . . . high levels. Evidence on the apparent beneficial effect of moderate drinking deserves acknowledgement and serious attention."

It was partly in response to Plant's outburst, and in the light of the new evidence about the health benefits of moderate drinking, that the Health Education Authority in Britain shortly afterwards began its review of the sensible drinking advice. But can "sensible limits" mean much? As Professor Plant told me, in most northern countries, including Canada, the United States, Scandinavia, and much of Britain, "the tradition has been to drink only to get intoxicated." That's one reason why those parts of the world have the highest heart attack rates. That and a taste for fatty foods.

Eric Appleby, head of the government-funded Alcohol Concern, believes many of Britain's drinking problems stem from what he calls, "the pub culture." He could equally have been talking about the North American bar scene. You know how it goes: half a dozen friends around the bar after work, lots of laughs and good cheer, and everyone pays for a round when it's their turn. In effect, the pace is set by the fastest drinker. So who says, "Enough!"? Too often nobody does. The result: binge drinking, the most dangerous sort. The international

INTERSALT blood pressure study found that a binge, even if you haven't taken a drink in weeks, can send your blood pressure soaring. Also, as mentioned earlier, although the alcohol provides some initial protection, after a binge there's a rebound effect eighteen hours later when the platelets actually become "stickier." That could be the time for a heart attack or a stroke. (There's one exception to that rule. In a series of experiments with rats, Dr. Serge Renaud found the rebound effect did not occur with red wine.) It's also the after-work or weekend booze-up, of course, that puts drunks behind the wheel and leads to accidents and domestic and other violence.

ARF, like agencies in a number of countries, proposes a daily safe limit rather than a weekly tally. In addition to a ceiling of two drinks a day, with less for women, it also suggests that people abstain at least one day a week — a useful check, I guess, on whether you are becoming addicted to alcohol. The trouble is, alcohol is not like medicine. We don't measure out two spoonfuls from the bottle on rising.

"Drinking," says Robin Room, ARF's research vice president, "is a social activity. We all rise and fall together." Which suggests one of the most interesting potential controls of all: we set our drinking limits by the friends we keep. If it's to change, any good advice governments can offer has to encourage people in the direction of a European pattern of drinking — usually one that involves drinking wine with food. It's already happening. More and more people on both sides of the Atlantic and Pacific are switching to table wine, and tending to drink at home, and with meals.

Martha Sanchez-Craig is an ARF senior scientist who has written a book called *Saying When* on how to quit or cut down if you have a drinking problem. She introduced me to a different notion: drinking days. Most people don't drink every day

— they drink when the occasion offers. To meet that social drinking definition, ARF has developed an alternative set of guidelines:

(No more than one drink per hour.

(No more than four drinks for a man and three drinks for a woman on the days that you drink.

(And no more than twelve drinks a week.

(Do not drink daily.

It all sounds a bit complicated to remember at a cocktail party: "Now was that four drinks an hour with an extra one for leap year, or three drinks a week not including Saturday?" And, of course, its admonition not to drink daily flies in the face of the best scientific advice that regular and modest drinking provides the heart with optimum protection. Sanchez-Craig, unlike many of her colleagues in the addiction field, takes a tolerant attitude towards the occasional over-indulgence. It's only realistic, she says, to recognize that people drink too much once in a while — and it's not a great risk if they plan, for instance, not to drive.

"It's something all of us do now and then," said the Mexican-born researcher. "There are times of the year when people probably exceed the limits. But I think the majority of people drink sensibly." Of necessity, the ARF figures, like the British formula, are all "best guesses."

How did the Health Education Authority, for instance, come up with the magic figures of fourteen and twenty-one units? John Duffy, the statistician at the Alcohol Research Group and a colleague of Plant's in Edinburgh, says it was "seat of the pants stuff." He told Kathryn McWhirter at the London *Independent*, "The figures were based on the opinions of a bunch of doctors . . . along with anti-alcohol lobbyers, at a meeting. The women's limit was set at fourteen, not because of any study, but having hit on twenty-one for men, they thought, 'women are much more delicate, so let's go for fourteen.' Since then, the twenty-one and fourteen units have been set in tablets of stone."

It is, Duffy has said on another occasion, "ridiculous" to suggest people are in trouble if they go over these limits. There were, ostensibly, reasons for setting a lower target for women: because of their smaller build and the fact that their systems contain less water than men, they supposedly absorb alcohol quicker. That's the theory.

Linda Bisson at the University of California says it isn't necessarily so. "It's clear that on the basis of strict etiology, men should be able to tolerate higher levels of alcohol. In fact, many women seem to have less of a problem than men do." It may, she said, have something to do with genetics. So what's the scientific evidence on useful limits? There are anomalies in the findings. A few researchers suggest health benefits reach their peak at less than a drink every couple of days. The Danish study found it was only when a drinker reached a level of sixty-nine British units a week — equivalent to five pints of regular beer a day — that his health risks equalled those of a teetotaller. Below that level, the Danes said, the drinker was ahead of the abstainer.

The study of twelve thousand British male doctors, headed by Sir Richard Doll, found the maximum benefit at a level of twenty to twenty-nine units a week, suggesting you could drink up to five bottles of wine or fourteen pints of beer and still get the maximum benefit.

But in the main, the studies have been surprisingly consistent in identifying that "narrow window" of protection. The maximum benefit in terms of protecting against coronary heart disease and other diseases occurs at a level of one, two, or three drinks a day. "The evidence suggests," reported the always conservative Professor Michael Marmot and a colleague in 1991, "that two drinks a day are associated with no cardiovascular harm and may be protective against coronary heart disease."

In another of the most careful studies, Dr. Michael Gaziano, a cardiologist at Harvard Medical School, found that the best protection against heart attacks came at up to three drinks a day. Dr. Serge Renaud, whose study of the French Paradox has guided much of the debate, says two or three glasses of red wine a day is "perfect."

Of course, there is a comforting margin of error in all the studies. It's generally acknowledged that when people are asked how much they drink, most will underestimate — usually by about 50 percent. So if the study says people are getting maximum benefit at a reported two drinks a day, chances are they're drinking three.

What to Tell the Kids

Perhaps it was because her father was French Canadian. Growing up in San Francisco, Linda Bisson remembers that there was always wine or beer on the table. "There was no encouragement, nor discouragement," said the biochemist who heads the Department of Viticulture and Enology at the University of California at Davis. "When we were small, if you wanted a little bit you could have it. The advantage was that, when we reached the teen years, we didn't have any trouble with alcohol and drugs. Our friends too who had been raised that way didn't think, 'Wow! I can drink alcohol now. I've got to go on a drinking binge.' We just didn't have that desire."

In many developed countries, and nowhere more than in Canada and the United States, parents are in a state of panic over their teenaged children drinking. I suspect that not much more drinking — and maybe less — goes on in the teenage years now than when I was growing up in the 1950s. But in North America and now increasingly in Europe, a fatal ingredient has been added to the teenaged drinking equation: the car. The trouble starts when young parents move out to distant suburbs deluding themselves that, "it's a wonderful place to raise kids." These bleak, faraway settlements, in fact, are usually the worst places to raise kids, something the youngsters soon discover for themselves once they hit the teen years. The biggest drawback of the suburbs is that, unlike the city, there is no way to get around without a car. The result is that on any given weekend, especially in summer, you are liable to read that three, four, five, or six teenagers or more have been killed in yet another horrendous crash, inevitably in the early hours of Saturday or Sunday morning, and usually on a country road following a party.

The anger and feelings of helplessness have prompted parents to demand new laws — which attack exactly the wrong end of the problem. They demand that the drinking age be raised, sometimes to an unrealistic twenty-one. After prohibition failed so miserably as a social policy in the earlier part of the century, North Americans are now trying to impose it on young people who are old enough to vote, to fight for their country, to marry, and to raise families. And prohibition for the young is proving as ineffectual as it did during the original "great experiment." The misguided parents would, in fact, be better off campaigning for an increase in the ridiculously low driving age of sixteen, or perhaps considering a move back to the city, where their young people, even if they happened to overindulge, could still get home safely by taxi or public transport.

There is, though, another answer. An answer that I heard from nearly everyone I spoke to who has given thought to the healthy — and unhealthy — aspects of alcohol consumption and the young. The answer is to accustom children early to treat alcohol in a sensible and mature fashion. Young people get into trouble because alcohol is a novelty to them. A New Brunswick, New Jersey, study found that most drinking-and-driving accidents occur within two years of young people first being introduced to alcohol. Loading the volatile teenaged system with two new and exciting experiences at the same time — drinking and driving — is simply asking for trouble.

Dr. Wells Shoemaker, the California pediatrician who writes about the alcohol field, believes it is both simplistic and naive to think you are going to stop young people drinking. It's a truth that holds true in most countries. Alcohol Concern, in Britain, says 82 percent of boys and 77 percent of girls in England and Wales have their first "proper drink" by the age of thirteen. In Canada, on average, students first try alcohol in grade seven.

In the United States, the latest panic involves drinking on university campuses, with one study, which has been criticized as spurious and unprofessional, alleging that half the university students polled are binge drinkers prone to violence and vandalism, while 90 percent of on-campus rapes and violent crimes involve alcohol. Whatever the true figures, Dr. Shoemaker believes drinking problems among the young stem from making alcohol "a forbidden fruit," with all the mystery and allure that suggests. It was a revelation to him, he said, when he left California at nineteen to study in Florence for six months. At home he and his California classmates had been obsessed with "scoring" a six-pack of beer and then drinking it surreptitiously.

"In Italy, by contrast, a wine bottle sat on the table as part of the meal. Students could talk with each other and ... the wine sat there as an unpretentious bystander, matter of fact, take it or leave it, along with the bread, the grated cheese, the water glass, and the spoons. There was," he said, "no novelty in going behind the stadium to drink and act stupid, any more than one would sneak out and gobble up the *panini* rolls which were always there for the asking."

Italian children, said Dr. Shoemaker, learn from seeing their parents drinking sensibly. "It's an ideal model," he said. And they soon realize that, in that society, to be seen intoxicated is to be regarded as a "buffoon, a jerk. And no adolescent wants to be regarded as a jerk."

Demystifying alcohol must start in the home, says Dr. Shoemaker. If the child is growing up in the 5 to 10 percent of families where alcohol is a problem, then the cause is lost. But the pediatrician addresses himself to the other 90 percent where drink isn't a problem. Parents who are moderate drinkers, he suggests, should offer their growing youngsters small portions of wine or beer with the meal. This way they will become accustomed to the flavour, and won't have to seek it out on the sly. They will grow to accept drinking as a normal part of a moderate family meal.

It is not a new answer. In his 1983 study, "The Natural History of Alcoholism," George E. Vaillant wrote, "Introducing children to the ceremonial and sanctioned use of low-proof alcoholic beverages taken with meals in the presence of others ... would appear to provide the best protection against future alcohol abuse."

To people in the Mediterranean countries, the obsession of North American parents with their children's drinking must seem strange indeed. To them there is no answer other than to bring children up to be familiar with wine. Dun Gifford, the Boston lawyer who has made it his life's work to promote healthful diets like that enjoyed in Mediterranean countries, says the biggest mistake is to make alcohol seem "dangerous and exciting."

"In European countries they know wine is not a binge drink. It's a subject about which children should be educated," he said. "But the education should begin, not in the school, but in the home." Professor Serge Renaud agrees. "In Mediterranean countries," he told me, "we start to drink from childhood. I started to drink a bit of wine and water when I was twelve. Starting early in life with extremely moderate amounts is a good way to avoid the weekend drinking, the drunkenness and the accidents later on." It also, he added, puts youngsters on the way to enjoying the health protection that wine provides in adult life.

Should I Drink? A Test

To many people the question will seem superfluous. "Should I drink? I'm already drinking." In Canada, 82 percent of men and 73 percent of women drink. In mainland Britain, according to Professor Martin Plant, about 95 percent of men and 90 percent of women drink. In the United States, drinking is less common: only 68 percent of men and 47 percent of women drink. In the Deep South where, for instance, in Alabama only 30 percent of the population drinks, the Prohibition spirit is still very much alive.

For the nondrinker, the new evidence about possible life-saving health benefits deriving from moderate consumption of wine and other alcoholic beverages poses a real conundrum. Is it wise, after years of abstaining, to take up drinking? What are the risks? Most doctors, in their public utterances anyway, take the safe route. If you don't already drink, don't start now, they say. But what if the person making the decision has a history of heart disease in his or her family? Then it needs some careful thought. Because deciding to drink wine, say, after taking care of other heart-protective steps like stopping smoking, getting regular exercise, and eating a low-fat diet, could be a life-saver, cutting the risk of a heart attack by up to 50 percent. And even for the person who drinks already, it's legitimate to ask, should I continue to drink? Because there are people who simply should not drink. Here are some questions to help you make the decision whether you should drink or not:

(Is there a history of alcohol abuse in your family — a parent or a grandparent who couldn't handle alcohol?

(Have you ever had difficulty controlling your drinking?

(Are there powerful religious or community reasons for you not to drink?

(Do you suffer from high blood pressure, gout, ulcers, or diabetes?

(Do you have an addictive personality — whether it relates to smoking, coffee, excessive eating, or just about anything else?

(Do you take regular medications that might act adversely in the presence of alcohol?

⟨ Do you suffer from a physical or mental condition —
particularly manic depression — that could be aggravated
by drinking?

⟨ Are you a woman with a breast cancer risk in your
family — a mother, grandmother or sister who contracted
this disease? (See the section on cancer.)

Answering yes to any of these questions does not necessarily disqualify you from drinking moderately. Neither does not knowing the answers where medical matters are involved. In either case you would be well advised to consult your doctor before making any decision.

Then there are times when you definitely should not drink. Some are obvious. When you are planning on driving or operating machinery, for instance. Or when you're handling firearms or dangerous substances. It's also a very bad idea to drink before exercising because alcohol blocks your body's natural warning systems and you could easily overdo it and suffer a heart attack. Only very moderate drinking is advised during pregnancy (see the section on women and alcohol). To my mind the official "don't drink" lists generally miss one of the most important exclusions: never drink when you have sole responsibility for the welfare of children.

In drinking, too, we are our brother and sister's keeper. We are not only responsible for our own drinking, but also to some extent for how much our friends and guests drink. Some thoughts:

⟨ Right at the start of the evening, offer soft drinks or juices
so that your guests don't feel they're being awkward asking
for them.

(Be especially thoughtful of the "designated driver," seeing he or she has plenty of nonalcoholic alternatives.

(Whether you're out or at home, there should be no pressure on anyone to "have another."

(It's not a good idea to keep filling people's wine glasses — or your own — before they're empty. That way it's almost impossible to keep check on how much you're drinking.

(Don't rush the pace. Don't be too eager to call for another round or to take the bottle around. There's no rush.

(Order or serve food when you're drinking — double the pleasure, as well as the safety.

(Serve water to your guests with their drinks, especially later in the evening, so they don't quench their thirst with beer or wine just before hitting the road.

(Opt for low-alcohol beverages — table wines, standard rather than extra-strength beers — and be parsimonious with spirits.

(And be ready to provide a taxi home for any guest who shouldn't be driving.

With these points in mind, and with the studies and discussions with scientists and doctors related in this book also in mind, you are now ready to make your own decision. But you may still have questions. The following chapter sets out some commonly asked questions and attempts to answer them.

CHAPTER VIII

Your
Questions

You Were Asking

 I've heard that sulfites in wine can be dangerous. Is that true?

Sulfites are present in practically every fermented product. They are a natural by-product of fermentation. In wine-making sulfites are often added for a "clean" fermentation in which unwanted bacteria are destroyed. Yeast can tolerate the sulfites, so it is not affected. Without sulfites, wine production is a hit-or-miss affair in which the wine may well turn out vinegary.

Unfortunately, due to the indiscriminate use of sulfites, not only in wines but also in dried fruits and even as a "freshener" to spray on restaurant salad bars, an increasing number of people are becoming allergic to sulfites. In extreme cases, heavy exposure can even lead to death.

How do I know if I'm allergic to sulfites?

If you experience constricting or itchiness in the throat after eating dates or raisins or sweet white wine, you should see your doctor. White wine contains higher levels of sulfites than red wine, but if you have a serious allergy you should probably not consume wine at all.

If resveratrol or any of the other phenolic compounds in wine are so good for me, why don't they bring them out in pill form?

A French pharmaceutical firm has brought out an over-the-counter pill claiming it contains wine flavonoids. Its effectiveness is unproven. The fact is fermentation seems to be the process that releases resveratrol and other flavonoids in a form in which our bodies can absorb them. Any serious attempt to market resveratrol or other flavonoids as drugs, particularly in the United States, would probably entail ten or fifteen years of testing before the products reached the market. Meanwhile they are available in wine — a product that has been safety tested for thousands of years. The other reason a pill might be second best: it's estimated that at least half the protection against coronary heart disease is provided by the alcohol in the wine. That protection would just not be there in a pill.

If the flavonoids are in the skin of the grape, why not just eat grapes?

A lot of people ask Leroy Creasy, the Cornell University professor who made some of the early tests on resveratrol, that question. Most table grapes — usually sweeter, larger, and more blemish-free than those grown for wine — are grown in hot, sunny climates where resveratrol is usually absent. Even if it were found that certain table grapes contained useful flavonoids, there is another drawback. You would have to eat an awful lot of them to get the same benefit you would from a glass of wine, and because table grapes are 20 percent sugar, you would be taking on a good number of calories.

Wouldn't raisins do the job?

Again, raisins are sweet, and if you eat a lot of them you are adding calories. There's another problem: raisins are made by drying grapes in the sun. Resveratrol disappears in the strong sun, so even if the grapes contained it in the first place, the raisins wouldn't. An executive with one of the giants of the raisin business thought he had that problem licked when he called Professor Creasy. "Our raisins never see the sun," he said. Instead, they are dried in huge mechanical dryers. Creasy dutifully tested the firm's raisins and found some flavonoids. "But they're not a high source," he said. "You're better off drinking a little bit of wine."

What about grape juice?

Andrew Waterhouse, the California scientist, says, "Juices seem to be shockingly low in these [phenolic] compounds." And where resveratrol has been added to grape juice, it disappears within two weeks. It apparently needs the alcohol in the wine for stability.

I make my own wine. How can I be sure it will contain high levels of these chemicals that will protect me from heart disease?

Alex Karumanchiri of the Liquor Control Board of Ontario has studied the question. His view: Don't buy grape juice to make your wine; instead you should ask for crushed and sulfited grapes, which generally come in buckets, refrigerated. It's more trouble, involves an extra step pressing the grapes, and it's more expensive. It would also be wise to seek out Pinot Noir grapes, which are high in resveratrol, although they may be harder to find.

Isn't that a lot of extra trouble and expense?

You asked.

You advise a glass or two of wine a day, but doesn't that mean there's always some left in the bottle that won't be fit to drink later?

Linda Bisson at the University of California, Davis, says red wine will take some abuse and still be worth drinking. "If

I'm keeping a bottle of red until the following day, I just put the cork back in and put it in the refrigerator," she says. "Store it on a low shelf where it's not too cold, then pour your glass half an hour before you're ready to drink it. That will give it time to reach room temperature."

White wine, she suggests, really needs to be consumed within an hour of opening. If you're leaving wine for several days, or keeping it at room temperature, she suggests using a vacuum pump. These handy gadgets come with their own special corks. The pump removes oxygen from the bottle, halting any deterioration in the wine.

I like my wine white and sweet. But you only seem to talk about dry red wines. What am I supposed to do?

It's a fact: the flavonoids that protect us from illness are part and parcel of that special dry flavour of red wine. Some white wines have low concentrations of these phenolics, and eventually wineries may find ways of adding more to their white wines. In the meantime, Linda Bisson recommends, "Start with the sweet stuff certainly — and then move on. Tastes evolve when you drink wine." There's a place for white wines — they are lighter and more delicate. And with white wine, she says, it's easier to avoid a bad match between the food and the wine.

"Reds tend to be more food-specific. They can be very intense in flavour," she says. After a while you can match the wine to your mood. "I don't have a favourite. Sometimes when I'm eating I will absolutely have to have a Chardonnay [used in making white Burgundy]. And sometimes it will have to be a Zinfandel [a California red grape], even a white Zinfandel. It's all a matter of mood."

It seems that sediment in the bottom is the price we pay for wines that are highest in phenolics. How do I avoid the sediment getting into the glass?

The constant tipping back and forth of the bottle as you go from glass to glass is guaranteed to disturb the sediment. The best answer is to decant the wine. That way you leave the sediment in the bottle as well as allowing the wine to combine with oxygen, releasing a good deal of the flavour and aroma. George Soleas, chairman of the technical committee of the Canadian Wine Institute, recommends you decant red wine an hour before you plan to drink it. White wines — as well as very old wines — he suggests, should be consumed within the hour unless they are to lose a lot of their zing.

In *The World Atlas of Wine*, Hugh Johnson says many young wines improve immeasurably with decanting. His method of decanting: while the bottle remains in a tilted wine basket (allowing the sediment to settle in the bottom corner), withdraw the cork gently (without a final jerk), wipe the neck, lift out the bottle (still at an angle), and pour gently into your decanter or carafe until you see the sediment start to creep up the neck of the bottle. A candle or light behind the bottle helps you to judge the moment when to stop pouring. For an especially expensive wine, drain the bottle through a paper coffee filter to get the last drop.

Are old wines richer in phenolics?

Depends which ones you're looking for. California tests on an old wine showed it was high in quercetin, the cancer-fighting agent, and other phenolics. But a Toronto test on a vintage bottle of French wine showed it contained hardly any resveratrol. It could have been a question of storage: exposure to light can destroy resveratrol.

What time of day do most heart attacks happen?

Toronto cardiologist Dr. Anatoly Langer: "Typically a heart attack happens between 6 and 9 a.m., and often at home." As we stir into wakefulness, our nervous system is under pressure, kick-starting the body back into action. Blood pressure increases, and so does the potentially dangerous "stickiness" of the blood platelets. "Don't jump out of bed," advises Dr. Langer. "Take it easy in the morning." People who work nights, he says, experience the reverse pattern — their time of maximum risk is at the end of the day, when they're waking up.

So should I have a glass of wine first thing to protect against a clot?

Absolutely not. The best time to prepare for the bodily stress of the morning is — the night before. Doctors in the Netherlands reported in 1994 that patients who had wine with their evening meal initially showed mildly lower levels of t-PA, a so-called "clot-busting" protein that protects against blockages in the arteries. But by morning, the danger time, levels of t-PA as well as other anti-clotting agents were significantly elevated. Protection when you most need it.

I take aspirin regularly to ward off heart attacks. So is there really any benefit in drinking wine for the same purpose?

Aspirin is highly effective in preventing platelet coagulation and stopping clots before they can start. It doesn't, however, boost the "good" HDL and reduce "bad" LDL cholesterol, as wine or other alcoholic beverages will. Nor does aspirin work as an antioxidant, as red wine does.

Should I stop taking aspirin then?

Not at all. Research shows that aspirin and alcohol work together for a greater overall protective effect. A word of warning: aspirin can cause gastric bleeding in some people. Personally, I take a quarter of an aspirin every other day — supposedly enough still to provide the protective effect. If in doubt, speak to your doctor.

I take an estrogen supplement. But do I need it if I also have a glass of wine with dinner?

The phenolics in red wine boost estrogen levels. When the science is better understood it may be a legitimate choice: estrogen supplement or red wine. There is a slightly increased risk of breast cancer with estrogen supplement. The best information suggests no such risk for light wine drinkers. Don't make any decision without talking to your doctor.

I am diabetic. Should I drink to protect against coronary heart disease?

Diabetes is a serious risk factor for heart disease. At the same time, diabetics must be extra careful about consuming alcohol. The Canadian Diabetes Association advises you only drink when your diabetes is well controlled, that you should only drink with food, avoid sweet drinks, like fortified wines, liqueurs, or mixes, and observe moderation. Again, you need to balance the risks and benefits.

That said, there is an exploding interest among scientists in alcohol's apparent ability to prevent or stave off adult-onset (as opposed to juvenile) diabetes. Two American studies have now suggested a 40 percent lower incidence of adult-onset diabetes among moderate drinkers. Adult-onset diabetes occurs when the insulin in our blood becomes less effective; the body boosts insulin production, blood sugar levels rise, and fat deposition occurs. But the new studies indicate alcohol makes insulin more sensitive (and effective), halting or slowing the dangerous sequence. It's all very young science, but it's something that bears paying close attention to as more answers emerge.

I often seem to get headaches after drinking red wine. Is there a connection?

Dr. Vivette Glover at the Queen Charlotte and Chelsea Hospital in London, England, says this belief has been around for centuries, especially with regard to migraine headaches. So she and a team of researchers decided to put it to the test. Migraine patients who had complained of this effect were given either a Spanish Rioja wine or vodka and lemonade, both disguised as much as possible so they would not know what they were drinking. Nine out of the eleven drinking the wine got headaches, while none of the eight drinking vodka did.

Just to confirm, the team gave red wine to another team of migraine patients who had not reported a problem with red wine — and none of them got headaches. The group has also shown in the test tube and with volunteers that red wine can release 5HT, a chemical implicated in causing headaches and migraines. Further tests showed that it was the flavonoids in the red wine that were to blame for the headaches.

Does that mean I should forget about drinking red wine for heart protection?

Alex Karumanchiri says he frequently hears this question from customers. In his experience, wines from different regions seem to affect people differently. Rhône wines, for example, seem more prone to trigger headaches. So he suggests people take the experimental approach. "Pick a wine from a good area, say a Bordeaux, and pour yourself a third of a glass," he says. "If it doesn't give you a headache, try a third of a glass each day for a few days, gradually building up to a glass. If you get a headache, try a wine from a different region, and gradually create a list of wines you can tolerate. I have many calls or letters from people thanking me because they can now enjoy red wines."

I have a prostate condition. Should I drink wine?

Your doctor may advise against it on the grounds that alcohol may act as an irritant and cause you even more discomfort. Interestingly, if you drink wine or beer on a regular basis, you are less likely to have an obstruction of this sort in the first place. A long-term study of seven thousand Japanese-American men on the Hawaiian island of Oahu, published in the journal *Prostate*, found that men who were moderate consumers of wine beer, or the rice wine sake (but not spirits) were significantly protected against obstructive uropathy. Obstructive uropathy usually refers to the blockage caused by the swollen prostate, a condition that gives older men that familiar middle-of-the-night, "I-gotta-go-but-I-can't-go" feeling.

My grandmother always said, for a cold, take aspirin, a hot toddy, and off to bed. Was she right?

Who would want to argue with a grandmother! Her advice is probably sound — although she may be a little late with the hot toddy. Scientists at the now-disbanded Common Cold Unit in Salisbury, England, recorded the drinking habits of 391 volunteers, then dropped various cold viruses into their nasal passages. Seems like a mean trick, but the outcome was surprising. Subjects who regularly consumed one or two drinks a day were 65 percent less likely to develop cold symptoms than abstainers, while those downing two or three drinks a day had an 85 percent advantage over nondrinkers. The researchers, Dr. David Tyrrell and Dr. Sheldon Cohen, speculated that alcohol may reduce the inflammation of the nasal passages caused by the virus, or may act directly to neuter the virus. Oh, I almost forgot. The whole advantage was wiped out for the moderate drinkers who also smoked. Sorry.

I've heard that alcohol relieves constipation.

Wouldn't you know it — there's even an elaborate study that's been conducted on this unappetizing topic. Dr. Christopher Probert told the British Society of Gastroenterology in 1994 that a moderate amount of alcohol acts as a mild laxative. On average, it takes food fifty-two hours to pass through our bodies in the case of men, and sixty hours for women. But, after checking with 676 men and 883 women, Dr. Probert found that, for those taking over four British alcohol units a day (about 2.5 to 3 regular drinks) the time was cut to an average of forty-nine hours. For those consuming under two units (about 1.5 drinks), the figure was fifty-four hours, and men experienced the most pronounced effect. Surprisingly, alcohol speeded up the process to a greater degree than the much-vaunted dietary fibre.

When I spoke to my doctor about drinking modest amounts of wine to help my heart, he pooh-poohed the idea that wine and alcohol can do you any good. What should I do?

Many doctors, trying to keep up with medical knowledge on so many fronts, have either ignored or are still in ignorance of the mounting scientific evidence on the health benefits of moderate wine and alcohol consumption. So when a patient asks, they tend to conceal their lack of knowledge by saying, "Oh, there's nothing in that." The best answer is to prepare yourself with scientific questions, perhaps gleaned from this book, that you can ask your doctor. Then you are in a better position to judge his or her knowledge and make a sensible decision.

I have a favourite California red, but I have no idea if it's high in flavonoids. How can I find out?

Write to the winery. You'd be surprised how pleased most wineries are when their customers take an interest in the product. Even if the winery can't give a specific answer, your letter will have served a purpose in making the winemaker aware consumers are interested in the health issue. And it may encourage them to use the best grapes and to discard practices like heavy filtering that reduce the flavonoid content.

How many years extra life will I gain by drinking moderately?

And how long is a piece of string? Andrew Waterhouse, the University of California scientist, says moderate wine consumption may boost life expectancy three or four years. But that's not the important point. The biggest loss, where coronary heart disease is concerned, comes as a result of people, men especially, dying in mid-life. Two years extended life when you're seventy-five may seem just dandy if you're on the receiving end. But, in the larger scheme of things, twenty or thirty years of productive life for a dad of forty-five is a much bigger payoff.

Agenda

In South Wales, where my parents grew up in the early part of this century, the chapel folk knew two things: that drink was the invention of the Devil, and that to put a foot inside a public house was to risk eternal damnation. We're more sophisticated these days. Not even modern-day prohibitionists would use words like that. But the chapel darkness of South Wales lingers on around the world. These days the message comes wrapped in social work jargon mouthed by international bureaucrats. But it is still the same message that was thundered from a thousand pulpits: drinking is an evil and an abomination and should be stopped if at all possible.

Disguised as advice given for the good of your health, it is much more effective than the old, Bible-thumping prohibitionism. Many people for whom moderate drinking presented no risk have been intimidated into abstinence, and the worldwide drop in alcohol and even wine consumption is a consequence. There is an extra edge of cynicism to the prohibitionist message today: the educated, well-paid addiction professionals know very well that for the vast majority of drinkers, the health benefits of moderate alcohol consumption far outweigh the dangers of overindulgence. That's not to say there are not people who shouldn't drink, and it is not to minimize the damage alcohol abusers do — not only to themselves, but to others too. But the hypocrisy has to stop. The evidence cannot be denied. Drinking in moderation is one of the best things you can do to prevent coronary heart disease, and drinking wine regularly is likely to improve your health in a number of areas.

The world needs to adjust to this new knowledge. As the more thoughtful people quoted in this book recognize, what's needed now is a dual approach to the drinking issue: for the minority who can't handle alcohol, we need to provide the strongest possible education programs to get them to cut down or stop drinking; and for the 90 percent or more who have no problem drinking in moderation, we need to get across the message that by consuming wine especially they are not only adding to life's pleasures, but also reducing their chances of having a heart attack by 40 percent or better.

More than that, the new knowledge about the health benefits of moderate drinking must be taken into account whether in setting new research targets or disposing of puritan laws that actually threaten people's health.

Research is the place to start. Two Dutch researchers, after studying more than four thousand scientific papers on alcohol consumption in 1993, found that only 7 percent were devoted to the effects of drinking at "sensible" levels. Top people in the research field, particularly in Canada and the United States, told me it is almost impossible to get government funding for projects that might produce some good news about alcohol's benefits. Nearly all the money goes to researchers adding to the familiar litany of alcohol's evils.

That's not to suggest that research into alcoholism should stop. But there are two sides to the coin. And the life-saving potential for the vast majority of moderate drinkers outweighs the risks for the few. Governments should not be pressing people to drink. But at the same time, in developed countries they should be making people aware, especially those in the high-risk categories, of the possible penalties of abstaining. The elderly especially need to know that moderate drinking is likely to do them good, not only in a social sense, but in reducing the risks of crippling or fatal heart disease. Doctors — the ones who know most about alcohol's benefits, and yet who are often reluctant to speak about them to their patients — should be encouraged to talk about alcohol, just as today they talk about exercise and diet.

In all countries too, instead of the dire warnings we've become accustomed to on half the products we consume, labels on wine, beer, and spirits should be permitted to extol the legitimate, life-saving benefits of these beverages. Professor David Goldberg foresees the day, for example, when wine labels will carry information on the flavonoid content of the wine.

In taxation terms, governments should stop regarding alcoholic beverages as milch cows to be taxed endlessly on the principle that they are harmful and dangerous. Wine in particular should be given relief, and the sensible consumption of wine — at home and with meals — should be actively promoted. Certain countries need to address specific, wrong-headed official attitudes towards moderate alcohol consumption. American and Canadian communities that have fallen under the sway of the panic-mongers on the fetal alcohol syndrome issue, for example, should immediately repeal laws requiring frightening and misleading signs about birth defects. Similarly, Washington should act to abolish the odious and deceptive warnings it now requires on bottles and in drinking establishments.

Most Canadian provinces should follow the lead of Britain and the province of Alberta, and allow the sale of wine in supermarkets. Nothing, in the long run, is more likely to associate wine in the public mind with food and sensible consumption.

It would be nice if governments and the medical profession took some of the steps I've proposed. Not to help the wine industry, which can look after itself, but because the sensible consumption of alcoholic beverages, and wine in particular, could extend and improve the quality of life for millions! I'm not holding my breath. The fears of some doctors and addiction professionals — some quite understandable — and the power, especially in North America, of the neo-prohibitionists have the effect of paralyzing government on the alcohol issue.

Happily the chance to protect ourselves against coronary heart disease and other illnesses through moderate wine consumption does not depend on the whim of governments. All that's needed is for people to hear the facts — through newspaper articles, radio and television shows, and books like this. And then they can make up their own minds.

INDEX

aspirin, protective effects of, 19, 224–25
  and alcohol consumption, 22, 225,
    228
Aspler, Tony, 128, 145, 146
atherosclerosis, 3, 5, 28, 29, 31, 46–47,
    80, 88, 89, 92, 102, 109, 113–14,
    117, 125, 159, 169
Atkin, Tim, 128
Auckland (New Zealand), 56, 57
Australia
  alcohol consumption in, 23, 75–76
  alcohol research in, 15–16
  calculating alcohol intake, 202
  CHD death rates in, 44, 44 fig.
  wine consumption in, 76
  wine industry in, 111, 121, 124 fig.
  wines from, 141–42
Austria
  CHD death rates in, 28 fig., 43, 44,
    44 fig.
  wine consumption in, 72 fig.

B

"bad" cholesterol. See LDL cholesterol
Baird, Ian, 88
Banting, Frederick, 109
Banting Institute (Toronto), 109
Beaujolais (wine region), 124 fig.,
    130–31
beer, 3, 44, 46, 48, 49, 50, 61, 73, 74,
    76, 86, 87, 161, 166, 184, 185,
    195, 198
Beijing (China), 56, 57
Belfast (Northern Ireland), 56, 58, 84
Belgium, CHD death rates in, 28 fig.,
    44 fig.
beta-carotene, 81, 83
"Bible Belt" (U.S.), 54
binge drinking, 4, 23–24,196, 203,
    204–5, 210
birth control pill, 157
birth defects, 162, 169, 170, 171
Bisson, Linda, 170, 207, 208–9, 221–22
blood cholesterol. See cholesterol
blood pressure, 39, 58, 157, 158, 205
  See also hypertension
Bordeaux (wine region), 51, 111, 121,
    124, 131–33
Boston University School of Medicine, 14
"boutique wines," 116
breast cancer, 35, 66, 97, 98, 166–68,
    169, 170–71, 214, 225

breast-feeding, 168, 177
Britain. See United Kingdom
British Columbia, wines from, 135
British Department of Transport, 199
British Heart Foundation, 88
British Journal of Addiction, 175
British Medical Journal, 50, 174, 181
British Ministry of Agriculture,
  Fisheries and Food, 82
British Regional Heart Study (1988),
    18–19
British Society of Gastroenterology, 228
Broken Cord (Michael Dorris), 172
Busseltown study (Australia, 1982), 15
Bulgaria, CHD mortality in, 28 fig.
  wines from, 148
BUPA (labs, U.K.), 79, 85
Burgundy (wine region), 51, 110, 111,
    121, 128–29
Burns, George, 181–82
bypass surgery. See coronary bypass
  surgery

C

California (wines), 49, 93, 94, 110, 111,
    114, 121, 123, 124 fig., 229
  regulations, alcohol consumption, 163
  wines from, 124 fig., 137–39
  resveratrol content of, 105, 137–40
  See also Napa Valley
California Department of Health
  Services, 179
Camargo, Carlos A., 156
Cambridge University, 37
Canada
  alcohol consumption in, 23, 75, 212
  CHD death rates in, 2, 28, 28 fig.,
    35, 43, 44, 44 fig., 165, 204
  drinking patterns in, 204
  fat consumption in, 58
  wine consumption in, 54, 71,
    72–73, 75, 76
  wine industry in, 111
  wines from, 124 fig., 134–36
  wine sales in, 55
Canadian Atherosclerosis Society, 108
Canadian Diabetes Association, 225
Canadian Wine Institute, 108, 123, 223
canola oil, 70
cancer, 15, 16, 62, 65, 73, 79, 82,
    96–98, 103, 113, 117, 153

and alcohol consumption, 3, 4,
162–68, 200
geophysical factors, 165
risk factors, 166
See also specific types
cancer of the larynx, 163, 164
cancer of the pharynx, 163
carcinogens, 164, 165
cardiac arrest, 32, 33, 34
cardiovascular death trends
international comparisons, 28, 28
fig., 44, 44 fig., 56–57
and wine consumption, 7, 87
See also specific countries
cardiovascular disease
ethno-cultural variables, 28–29
and heredity, 39
and moderate alcohol consumption,
3, 194
Cardiovascular Review Group (U.K.), 87
Catalonia (Spain), 56, 84
catechin (antioxidant), 104, 105–6,
113, 114, 115, 117, 138
See also epicatechin
Central Europe, wines from, 148
Center for Science in the Public
Interest (U.S.), 162
cerebral embolism, 153
cerebral hemorrhage, 154
cerebral thrombosis, 153
CHD. *See* coronary heart disease
Chicago Board of Health, 180
Chile
wine consumption in, 72 fig.
wine industry in, 121
wines from, 147–48
chill filtering, 115–16
China, 91
diet in, 64, 97
tobacco consumption in, 56
cholesterol, 29–31, 35, 38, 39, 46, 58,
88, 89
and cardiovascular disease, 29
ratios, importance of, 30, 39
See also fats; HDL cholesterol; LDL
cholesterol
choosing healthful wines, guidelines,
121–49
Churchill, Sir Winston, 34–35
cirrhosis of the liver, 4, 13, 14, 20, 61,
165, 198
cis-resveratrol, 112, 124 fig., 127

clogging of arteries. *See* atherosclerosis
clot-caused strokes. *See* ischemic stroke
Cohen, Sheldon, 228
colds, 228
colon cancer, 97, 100
Committee on the Medical Aspects of
Food Policy (COMA) (U.K.), 68,
103, 191
Common Cold Unit (Salisbury, U.K.), 228
constipation, 186, 228–29
cooking methods, importance of, 66
Copenhagen (Denmark), 49
Cork, Margaret, 199
Cornell University, 89, 90, 123, 131,
140, 220
coronary artery disease, 32, 53, 160
coronary bypass surgery, 32, 102
coronary heart disease (CHD), 33–34,
35, 43, 55, 64, 82, 84, 153
and beer consumption, 44, 48, 49,
50, 61
and blood pressure, 39, 58
and diet, 20, 28, 39, 40, 58–59, 67
international comparisons, 54,
56–57, 60
and moderate alcohol consumption,
2, 20, 22, 40, 43, 58, 61, 83, 108,
154, 156, 169, 191–92, 193, 194,
195, 231, 234
rates (by country), 44, 44 fig.
risk factors, 157
and spirits consumption, 44, 45, 48,
49, 50
and stress, 37
Creasy, Leroy, 90, 104, 107–8, 109, 112,
123, 131, 140, 220, 221
Creasy, Minn, 109
Czechoslovakia (former), CHD mortality
in, 28 fig.
Crete, diet in, 66, 70
Criqui, Michael, 195–97

D
Dahl, Peter, 161–62
Daily Telegraph (London), 52, 59–60
Danish Epidemiological Science
Centre, 49
Davis (California; wine research),
101–6, 108, 114
death rates. *See* cardiovascular death
trends
decanting wine, 223

INTERSALT blood pressure study
(Marmot, 1994), 201, 205
Ireland, CHD death rates in, 28 fig.,
43, 44, 44 fig.
See also Northern Ireland
Irex, John, 107–8, 110, 116
ischemic stroke, 15, 20, 153, 156
Israel, CHD death rates in, 28 fig.
See also Tel Aviv
Italy
alcohol consumption in, 23, 211
CHD death rates in, 28 fig., 43, 44,
44 fig., 60, 143
CHD levels in, 23
diet in, 56
wine consumption in, 72
wine region, 124 fig.
wines from, 143–44

J
Jackson, Rodney, 16
Japan, 91
alcohol research in, 92, 94–95, 109
all-cause mortality in, 195
CHD death rates in, 28 fig., 60, 196
Jefferson Medical College
(Philadelphia), 163
Johnson, Hugh, 223
Journal of Substance Abuse, 184
J-shaped curve, 13, 154, 160
See also U-shaped curve
junk food, 65

K
Kaiser Permanente Medical Center
(Oakland, California), 15
Kaplan, George A., 179
Karumanchiri, Alex, 7, 107–8, 109–10,
112, 115, 116, 123–24, 137,
221, 227
Kastenbaum, Robert, 180
Khaw, Key-Tee, 37
Klatsky, Arthur, 14–15, 17–18, 43, 45,
48–49, 67–68, 69–70, 155,
160–61, 181, 201
Klein, Hugh, 184
Klurfeld, David, 46–47
Knupfer, Genevieve, 175
"kojo-ken" (Japan, folk medicine), 91, 92
Korea, folk medicine in, 91–92

Koren, Gideon, 175
Kritchevsky, David, 46–47

L
labelling, 135, 137, 144, 162, 171, 233
Lancet, The, 19, 45, 57, 195
Langer, Anatoly, 27, 31, 32, 33, 34, 224
LCBO. See Liquor Control Board of
Ontario
LDL cholesterol, 2, 3, 30–31, 38, 39,
65, 66, 82, 83, 88, 93, 104, 105,
112, 117, 138, 225
Lee, Philip, 199
Leighton, Terrance, 96–101
Lian, Camille, 159
life expectancy. See longevity
lifestyle, 5, 6, 28, 37, 38, 70
Lille (France), 56
liquor. See spirits
Liquor Control Board of Ontario, 7,
107, 110, 111, 123, 221
liver cancer, 163, 164, 165
liver cirrhosis. See cirrhosis of the liver
longevity, 2, 5, 7, 12, 33, 62, 82, 196,
230, 234
Longnecker, Matthew, 167
lung cancer, 11, 164, 166, 170
Luxembourg, wine consumption in, 72
Lyon Cardiovascular Hospital, 62

M
McWhirter, Kathryn, 206
mammogram, 167
Manchester University, 45
manic depression, 214
Marmot, Michael, 191–92, 193, 201, 208
Mattivi, Fulvio, 112, 114, 143
Maury, Emmerick, 185
Maxwell, Simon, 85–86, 87, 105
Medical Research Council (Cardiff,
Wales), 43
Medicinal Virtues of Alcohol in
Moderation Conference (1991,
Sydney, Australia), 11
Mediterranean diet, 62–71, 143
components of, 62–63, 66
nutritional pyramid, 67 fig., 68
men
cardiovascular death trends among,
28, 35, 36 fig., 44
and CHD mortality, international
comparisons, 56, 57
and diet, 37

and heart attack
  critical age for, 4–5, 29, 35, 89,
    169, 200
  Monica study, 56, 57
  risk factors, 38
menopause, 5, 29, 30, 35, 38, 89, 167,
  169, 170, 181, 186, 200
migraine headache, 226
Monica study (1985–95), 55–57,
  59–60, 193
mortality rates
  compared to alcohol consumption,
    12–13, 13 fig., 195–96
  male/female (1992), 28, 28 fig.,
    36 fig.
Mothers Against Drunk Driving, 162
mouth cancer, 163, 164
myocardial ischemia. See angina

N
Napa Valley (California), 116, 138, 161
narrowing of the arteries.
  See atherosclerosis
National Cancer Institute, 166
National Health Service (U.K.), 46
National Institute of Health (Maryland),
  97, 184
National Institute of Health and
  Nutrition (Tokyo), 88
National Institute on Aging, 179
natural foods, 28
"The Natural History of Alcoholism"
  (George Vaillant), 211
neo-prohibitionists, 162–63, 176, 231, 234
Netherlands
  alcohol research in, 22–23, 84,
    224, 232
  CHD death rates in, 28 fig., 44,
    44 fig.
Newcastle (Australia), 56, 57
New England Journal of Medicine (NEJM),
  18, 166
New York wines, 93, 94, 107, 135,
  139–41
New Zealand
  CHD death rates in, 44, 44 fig.
  alcohol research in, 16
  wine industry in, 111
  wines from, 142–43
Niagara region (Ontario), wines from,
  121, 124, 135

Ninewells Hospital (Dundee), 60
North America, cardiovascular disease
  trends, 3–4, 8, 28–29, 28 fig.,
    36 fig., 165
North American–style diet, 29, 46–47,
  54, 65, 75, 105, 106
Northern Ireland
  diet in, 66
  CHD death rates in, 28 fig.
Norway, CHD death rates, 44, 44 fig.
nutri-ceuticals, 98, 101
nutrition. See diet

O
obesity, 39, 70, 103, 159, 183, 186
Oldways Preservation and Exchange
  Trust, 64, 67 fig., 68, 69
olive oil, 62, 63, 65–66, 68, 69, 70
Ontario, wines from, 134–36
Ontario Wine Council, 134
oral cancers, 163, 164, 200
Oregon, wines from, 121, 124 fig.,
  136–37
osteoporosis, 181, 185–86
Oxford University, 11
oxidation, 79, 80, 83, 104

P
Pasteur, Louis, 6
Pauling, Linus, 81
Pearl, Raymond, 12, 13
Perold, Abraham Izak, 145
Perth (Australia), 56, 57
Peto, Richard, 19
phenolics, 7, 22, 95, 100, 106, 109, 111,
  112, 114, 115, 116, 222, 223–24
Pittman, David J., 184
Plant, Martin, 203–4, 206
Plant, Moira, 168, 173, 174, 176–78, 203
Poland, CHD death rates in, 28 fig.
Portugal
  CHD death rates in, 28 fig.
  wine consumption in, 72 fig.
  wines from, 144–45
pregnancy, and alcohol consumption,
  162, 168, 171–78, 187
  safe drinking limit, 175, 214
Prentice, Andrew, 182–84
Probert, Christopher, 228
processed foods, 105
Prohibition, 71, 72, 209, 213